# CROSS STITCH
## FOR
# SPECIAL OCCASIONS

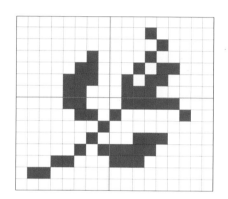

# CROSS STITCH
## FOR
# SPECIAL OCCASIONS

### OVER 30 EASY-TO-MAKE PROJECTS

### MARIA KELLY

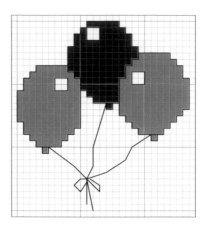

First published in Great Britain in 2000 by
Collins & Brown Ltd
London House
Great Eastern Wharf
Parkgate Road
London SW11 4NQ

Distributed in the United States and Canada by Sterling Publishing Co.,
387 Park Avenue South, New York, NY 10016, USA

1 3 5 7 9 8 6 4 2

British Library Cataloguing-in-Publication Data:
A catalogue record for this book is available from the British Library.

ISBN 1 85585 780 4

EDITORIAL DIRECTOR: Sarah Hoggett
EDITOR: Clare Churly
DESIGNER: Claire Graham
PHOTOGRAPHY: Jon and Barbara Stewart

This book was typeset using Baskerville and Bembo.

# Contents

Introduction  6

## New Baby  8

*New-born Baby Card*  10  •  *Teddy Bear Shawl*  12
*Animal Ark Sampler*  16  •  *Bunny Rabbit Bib*  20

## Birthdays  22

*21st Birthday Card*  24  •  *Gift Tags*  26  •  *60th Birthday Sampler*  30
*Jewellery Box*  34  •  *Sports Theme Birthday Card*  38
*Floral Birthday Card*  40

## Christenings  42

*Christening Photograph Frame*  44  •  *Butterfly Shawl*  48
*Christening Gown*  52  •  *Photograph Album Cover*  54
*Cake Band*  60  •  *Christening Sampler*  62

## Engagements & Weddings  66

*Engagement Card*  68  •  *Wedding Cake Card*  70
*Wedding Bouquet Sampler*  72  •  *Scented Wedding Shoe Cushion*  76
*Wedding Ring Cushion*  80  •  *Bridesmaid's Dress*  84
*Drawstring Bag*  88  •  *Wedding Photograph Frame*  92

## Anniversaries  96

*Silver Wedding Card*  98  •  *Golden Wedding Sampler*  100
*Ruby Wedding Photograph Frame*  104  •  *Family Tree Sampler*  108
*Anniversary Photograph Album Cover*  112

Alphabets and Templates  116
Basic Materials and Techniques  122
Index  127
Acknowledgements  128

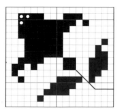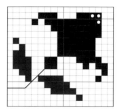

# Introduction

One of my most treasured childhood memories is of receiving a beautiful sewing box as a birthday present. I remember opening the box and finding surprise upon surprise inside: a thimble, a packet of needles, scissors, skeins of threads in a beautiful rainbow of colours, and a neatly folded placemat stamped with a cross stitch design.

This placemat was to be my first attempt at cross stitch. Being a rather head-strong little girl, I would not allow my mother to help me. I therefore started by threading all six strands of the thread on to my needle. This, as you can imagine, took some time! Still, thread them I did, and I proceeded to cross stitch.

The crosses went in any way I felt inclined to stitch them at the

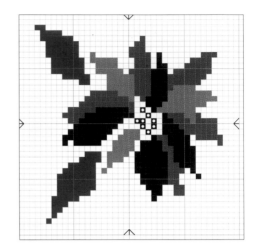

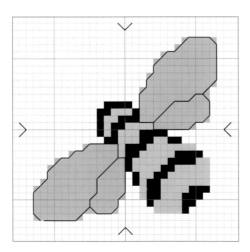

time – and as for the back! Well, the least said the better.

When I finished I proudly presented the placemat to my mother. She, of course, had to put it on display, but finding the right place for this wonderful piece of embroidery was no easy feat. The placemat, with its six-strand thread plus its knots and loops, would allow nothing to sit flat, and photograph frames always tilted and fell over when stood upon it.

My first example of cross stitch would certainly have received no prizes, but the joy I experienced as I completed each flower and leaf cannot be taken away. I have come on a little since then, my crosses now all go in the same direction and there are no knots and loops, but the one constant is that the pleasure still remains.

Having a completely blank piece of fabric and watching the design begin to grow, stitch upon stitch, still fills me with awe.

I do hope that you will use the designs in this book to mark those special and wondrous events in your life, and in the lives of those near and dear to you. Nothing can achieve a sense of affection like a gift that has been stitched with love. I have tried to give the designs an intimate feel, as I believe that many will become windows to a family's history for the generations to come.

Happy stitching.

*Maria Kelly*

# New Baby

# New-born Baby Card

*Celebrate the birth of a girl or boy with this lovely card.
The centre of the design is a beautiful old-fashioned pram,
and around this are a wealth of baby motifs such as building
blocks, bootees and even a knitted hat.*

## MATERIALS

- 1 piece of 18ct white Aida
10 in x 8 in (25.5 cm x 20.5 cm)

- 29 in (74 cm) of yellow and
white gingham ribbon ½ in
(1.5 cm) wide

- 4 yellow buttons

- 1 white greetings card blank
with rectangular opening
measuring 5¾ in x 3¾ in
(14.5 cm x 9.5 cm)

- Double-sided adhesive tape

- 1 skein of each of the
following colours of thread:

DMC 818 pale shell pink

DMC 760 mid apricot
pink

DMC 744 mid corn yellow

DMC 598 turquoise

DMC 340 mid lilac

DMC 413 very dark grey

## METHOD

**1** To prevent the fabric edges from fraying, neaten by either taping with masking tape or hemming.

**2** Locate the centre of the fabric by folding in half horizontally and vertically. You may find it easier to mark the fold lines by tacking with a contrasting thread. Use a hoop or frame to help keep the tension even and the fabric taut (see page 123).

**3** Locate the centre of the design using the arrows at the edge of the chart. Begin at the centre of the design with your first cross stitch and continue working outwards.

**4** Stitch using two strands of thread for cross stitch and two strands of thread for the french knots (see pages 125). Using DMC 413, backstitch the outlines with one strand of thread and the pram wheels, handlebars and the lettering with two strands. Long stitch the spokes of the pram wheels with two strands of DMC 413 and the hood supports with one strand of DMC 413.

### MAKING UP

**1** When the design is complete, remove the hoop or frame and press. If necessary, wash the fabric prior to pressing it.

**2** Attach double-sided tape to the front of the card ¼ in (5 mm) from the edge of the opening. Cut the ribbon so that it runs from one edge of the card to the other on each of

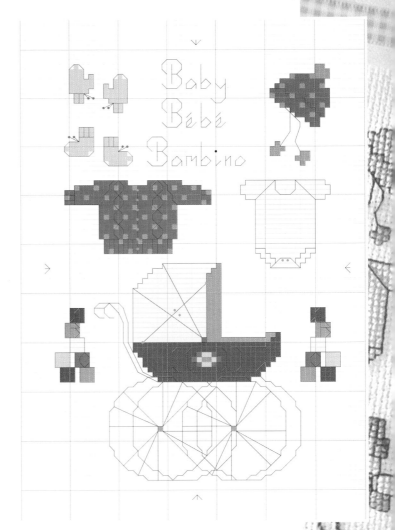

KEY TO CHART  • = French knot

the four sides. Stick the ribbon to the tape around the opening and cut the ribbon edges to an angle. Attach a button to each corner where the ribbons meet using glue or by stitching through the card and ribbon.

**3** Apply double-sided adhesive tape to the inside of the card around the edges of the opening. Position the Aida to ensure that the design is centred and stick down.

**4** Place double-sided adhesive tape around the inside of the card's left-hand flap and fold over to cover the back of the stitching.

# Teddy Bear Shawl

*This exquisite shawl is the perfect present for a new-born baby. Decorated with jolly teddy bears and balloons, the ABC motif will also prove useful when the child is old enough to learn to read.*

## MATERIALS

- 1 18ct Afghan shawl as large or small as you require

- 1 skein of each of the following colours of thread:

| | |
|---|---|
| ⬜ | DMC blanc |
| ⬜ | DMC 604 light pink |
| ⬛ | DMC 602 mid pink |
| ⬛ | DMC 601 deep pink |
| ⬛ | DMC 740 orange |
| ⬜ | DMC 725 yellow |
| ⬜ | DMC 677 straw |
| ⬜ | DMC 676 light gold |
| ⬛ | DMC 729 mid gold |
| ⬛ | DMC 3829 dark gold |
| ⬜ | DMC 800 light sky blue |
| ⬜ | DMC 809 mid sky blue |
| ⬛ | DMC 799 deep sky blue |
| ⬛ | DMC 413 very dark grey |
| ⬛ | DMC 310 black |

## METHOD

**1** Decide where you would like the embroidered teddy bears and balloons to appear on the shawl. Depending on your preferences, you can choose to embroider any combination of the motifs that appear on pages 14–15. Use a hoop or frame to help keep the tension even and the fabric taut (see page 123).

**2** Locate the centre of the design using the arrows at the edge of the chart. Begin at the centre of the design with your first cross stitch and continue working outwards.

**3** Cross stitch over two threads. Stitch using two strands of thread for cross stitch and two strands of thread for french knots (see page 125). Use one strand of DMC 413 for backstitching the outlines and details and use two strands for backstitching the balloon strings and the duck's lead.

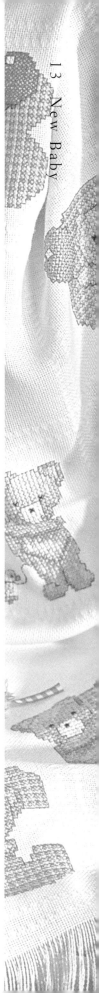

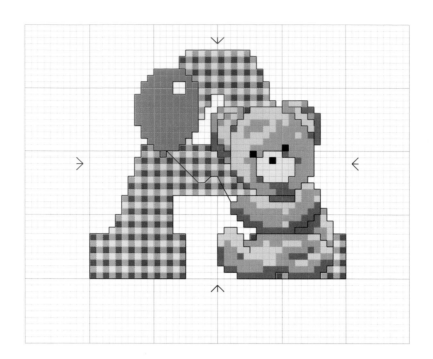

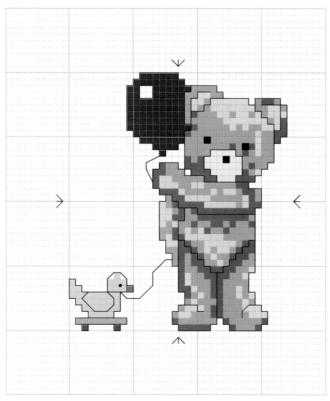

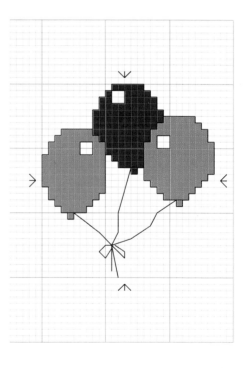

KEY TO CHART  ● = French knot

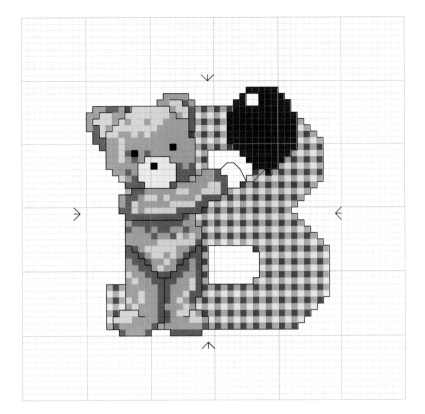

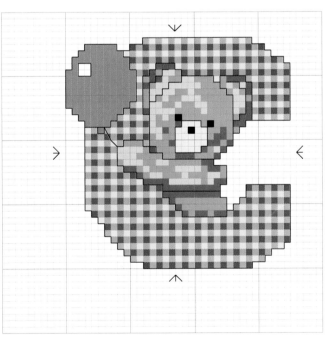

## MAKING UP

**1** When the embroidery is complete, remove the hoop or frame and press. If necessary, wash the embroidered shawl according to the manufacturer's instructions prior to pressing it.

**2** Pull away threads from the outside edges of the shawl until you have made a fringe that is 2½ in (6.5 cm) long.

# Animal Ark Sampler

*A hand-stitched Ark sampler is a special way to commemorate a child's birth. The bright colours and cheerful animals will make it popular with children of all ages and a must for the nursery.*

## MATERIALS

- 1 piece of 14ct white Aida 13 in x 14 in (33 cm x 35.5 cm)

- 1 skein of each of the following colours of thread:

|   |   |
|---|---|
| ☐ | DMC blanc |
| ☐ | DMC 605 candy pink |
| ◼ | DMC 350 orange/pink |
| ◼ | DMC 347 red |
| ☐ | DMC 725 yellow |
| ☐ | DMC 726 mid yellow |
| ◼ | DMC 977 light caramel |
| ◼ | DMC 976 mid caramel |
| ◼ | DMC 640 golden brown |
| ◼ | DMC 975 toffee brown |
| ◼ | DMC 911 mid green |
| ◼ | DMC 807 mid turquoise |
| ◼ | DMC 322 mid blue |
| ◼ | DMC 824 dark blue |
| ◼ | DMC 820 royal blue |
| ◼ | DMC 3746 purple |
| ☐ | DMC 415 light silver grey |
| ◼ | DMC 413 very dark grey |
| ◼ | DMC 310 black |

## METHOD

**1** To prevent the fabric edges from fraying, neaten by either taping with masking tape or hemming.

**2** Locate the centre of the fabric by folding in half horizontally and vertically. You may find it easier to mark the fold lines by tacking with a contrasting thread. Use a hoop or frame to help keep the tension even and the fabric taut (see page 123).

**3** Locate the centre of the design using the arrows at the edge of the chart. Begin at the centre of the design with your first cross stitch and continue working outwards.

**4** Stitch using two strands of thread for cross stitch and two strands of thread for french knots (see page 125). Use one strand of DMC 413 for backstitch, except for the lettering which requires two strands of thread. (You will find a chart for a complete alphabet on page 117.)

## MAKING UP

**1** When the design is complete, remove the Aida from the hoop or frame and press. If necessary, wash the fabric prior to pressing it.

**2** Stretch the fabric to ensure that it is taut and frame. Alternatively, take your sampler along to an experienced picture framer.

KEY TO CHART  • = French knot

# Bunny Rabbit Bib

*A decorated baby's bib is a fun project to make. This delightful design includes a cross stitch frieze of a toy train with rabbits riding in the wagons.*

## MATERIALS

- 1 18ct white Aida band with a yellow edge 1¾ in (4.5 cm) wide and 11 in (28 cm) long or as long as your bib requires

- 2 pieces of yellow and white gingham 11 in x 11 in (28 cm x 28 cm)

- 1 piece of firm interfacing 11 in x 11 in (28 cm x 28 cm)

- 27 in (70 cm) of yellow bias binding

- 1 skein of each of the following colours of thread:

  - DMC 3354 mid candy pink
  - DMC 666 orange/red
  - DMC 741 mid orange
  - DMC 726 mid yellow
  - DMC 988 mid green
  - DMC 995 turquoise
  - DMC 3746 purple
  - DMC 413 very dark grey

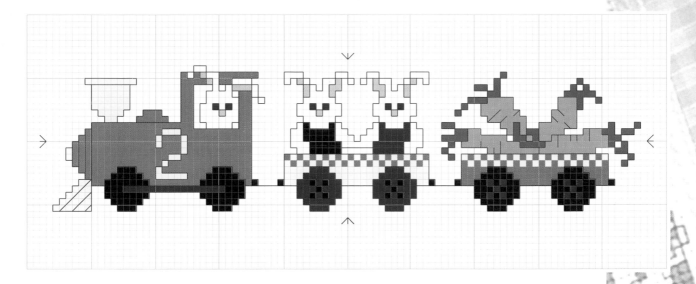

## METHOD

**1**  Locate the centre of the fabric by folding in half horizontally and vertically. You may find it easier to mark the fold lines by tacking with a contrasting thread. Use a hoop or frame to help keep the tension even and the fabric taut (see page 123).

**2**  Locate the centre of the design using the arrows at the edge of the chart. Begin at the centre of the design with your first cross stitch and continue working outwards.

**3**  Stitch using two strands of thread for cross stitch and one strand of DMC 413 for the backstitch.

## MAKING UP

**1**  When the design is complete, remove the hoop or frame and press. If necessary, wash the fabric prior to pressing it.

**2**  The instructions below tell you how to make a bib. If you don't want to make one yourself, you can use a white store-bought bib and attach the embroidery to it by following step 4 below.

**3**  Copy the pattern for the bib on page 121. Mark out the pattern on the interfacing and cut out once. Mark out the pattern on the gingham. Add ½ in (1 cm) to each side of the pattern beyond the marked edges and cut out twice.

**4**  Place the embroidered band on top of the right side of one of the gingham bib shapes. Carefully position the band 2 in (5 cm) from the bottom edge and tack in place. Machine stitch the band to the front of the bib.

**5**  Place the two gingham bib shapes right sides together and place the interfacing on top. Tack in place and machine stitch around the edges, leaving the neck edge open.

**6**  Snip around the edge of the bib to remove excess material and turn the bib right side out.

**7**  Tack the bias binding around the neck edge, allowing 9 in (23 cm) of binding for each of the bib ties. Ensure that all the raw edges are covered, machine stitch in place and iron.

# Birthdays

# 21st Birthday Card

*This coming-of-age card adds a personal touch to a special occasion. The traditional key symbol is combined with sophisticated cross-stitch decoration to create a fitting card for such an important day.*

## MATERIALS

- 1 piece of 14ct ivory Aida 8 in x 10 in (20 cm x 25 cm)

- 1 white greetings card blank with rectangular opening measuring 3½ in x 5½ in (9.5 cm x 14 cm)

- Double-sided adhesive tape

- 1 skein of each of the following colours of thread:

  DMC 798 sky blue

  DMC 5291 royal blue metallic

  DMC 415 light silver grey

  DMC 318 mid silver grey

  DMC 5287 dark grey metallic

  DMC 413 very dark grey

## METHOD

**1** To prevent the fabric edges from fraying, neaten by either taping with masking tape or hemming.

**2** Locate the centre of the fabric by folding in half horizontally and vertically. You may find it easier to mark the fold lines by tacking with a contrasting thread. Use a hoop or frame to help keep the tension even and the fabric taut (see page 123).

**3** Locate the centre of the design using the arrows at the edge of the chart. Begin at the centre of the design with your first cross stitch and continue working outwards.

**4** Stitch using two strands of thread for cross stitch and one strand of DMC 413 for the backstitch.

**5** Alternatively, if you want to celebrate an 18th birthday, you could replace the figure 21 with an 18. The chart above provides a pattern for both numbers.

## MAKING UP

**1** When the design is complete, remove the hoop or frame and press. If necessary, wash the fabric prior to pressing it.

**2** Apply double-sided adhesive tape to the inside of the card around the edges of the opening. Carefully position the embroidery to ensure that the design appears in the centre of the opening and stick down.

**3** Looking at the inside of the card, place double-sided adhesive tape around the inside of the bottom flap and fold the card over to cover the back of the embroidery.

# Gift Tags

*These lavishly embroidered gift tags are quick to make and perfect for decorating a special present. From a baby's rattle to a champagne bottle there are designs to suit every event.*

## MATERIALS

- ¼ of a sheet of 14ct clear plastic canvas per gift tag

- 1 piece of felt 5 in x 5 in (13 cm x 13 cm) per gift tag

- 10 in (25 cm) of ribbon ¼ in (5 mm) wide per gift tag

- Fabric glue

- 1 skein of each of the colours of thread specified on pages 28–9

## METHOD

**1** Locate the centre of the plastic canvas.

**2** Find the centre of your chosen design using the arrows at the edge of the chart. Begin at the centre of the design with your first stitch and continue to work outwards.

**3** Stitch using three strands of thread for cross stitch and one strand for backstitch.

## MAKING UP

**1** Carefully cut around the design leaving one row of plastic canvas squares from the edge of the stitching to the cut edge.

**2** Use the stitched embroidery as a template and cut out a piece of felt to cover the back of the tag.

**3** Form a loop with the ribbon and use fabric glue to stick it to the back of the embroidery in the desired place.

**4** Glue the front of the felt and press the sticky side of the felt to the back of the stitched gift tag.

## RATTLE GIFT TAG

- DMC 5288 pink metallic
- DMC 326 burgundy
- DMC 5279 rust metallic
- DMC 725 yellow
- DMC 954 light green
- DMC 911 mid green
- DMC 5290 turquoise metallic
- DMC 813 pale blue
- DMC 5289 purple metallic
- DMC 3799 charcoal grey

## BUMBLE BEE GIFT TAG

- DMC 725 yellow
- DMC 5283 platinum metallic
- DMC noir (black metallic)

## FLOWER GIFT TAG

- DMC blanc
- DMC 776 light pink
- DMC 899 mid pink
- DMC 3821 mustard yellow
- DMC 3820 dark mustard yellow
- DMC 563 light green
- DMC 562 mid green
- DMC 561 dark green

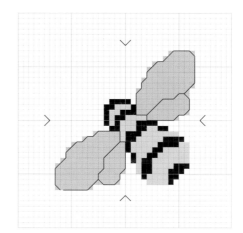

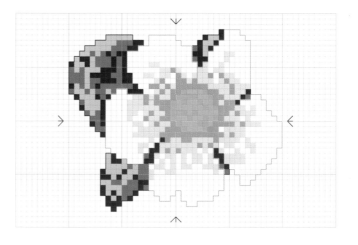

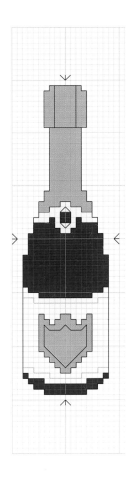

## CHAMPAGNE BOTTLE GIFT TAG

□ DMC ecru

▢ DMC 5284 gold metallic

■ DMC 3799 charcoal grey

■ DMC 310 black

## BIRTHDAY CUP CAKE GIFT TAG

▢ DMC 3708 mid pink

▢ DMC 956 pink

▢ DMC 741 mid orange

▢ DMC 725 yellow

□ DMC 744 mid corn yellow

■ DMC 632 brown

▢ DMC 826 blue

■ DMC 3799 charcoal grey

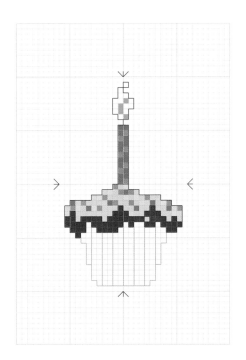

# 60th Birthday Sampler

*This specially designed 60th birthday sampler is ideal for anyone who has a passion for gardens and gardening. Fruit and vegetables, tools and flowers are all brought to life in colourful cross stitch.*

## MATERIALS

- 1 piece of 14ct white Aida 16 in x 17 in (40.5 cm x 43 cm)

- 1 skein of each of the following colours of thread:

  DMC blanc

  DMC 3688 mid pink

  DMC 3687 raspberry pink

  DMC 3803 aubergine

  DMC 3685 dark aubergine

  DMC 3350 magenta

  DMC 321 pillar-box red

  DMC 666 orange/red

  DMC 740 orange

  DMC 741 mid orange

  DMC 742 golden yellow

  DMC 3828 dark golden brown

  DMC 869 dark old gold

  DMC 420 mid old gold

  DMC 640 mid beige brown

  DMC 966 light mint green

  DMC 368 mid mint green

  DMC 989 light green

  DMC 988 mid green

  DMC 703 mid lime green

  DMC 986 dark green

  DMC 825 dark blue

  DMC 826 blue

  DMC 813 pale blue

  DMC 415 light silver grey

  DMC 318 mid silver grey

  DMC 414 dark silver grey

  DMC 413 very dark grey

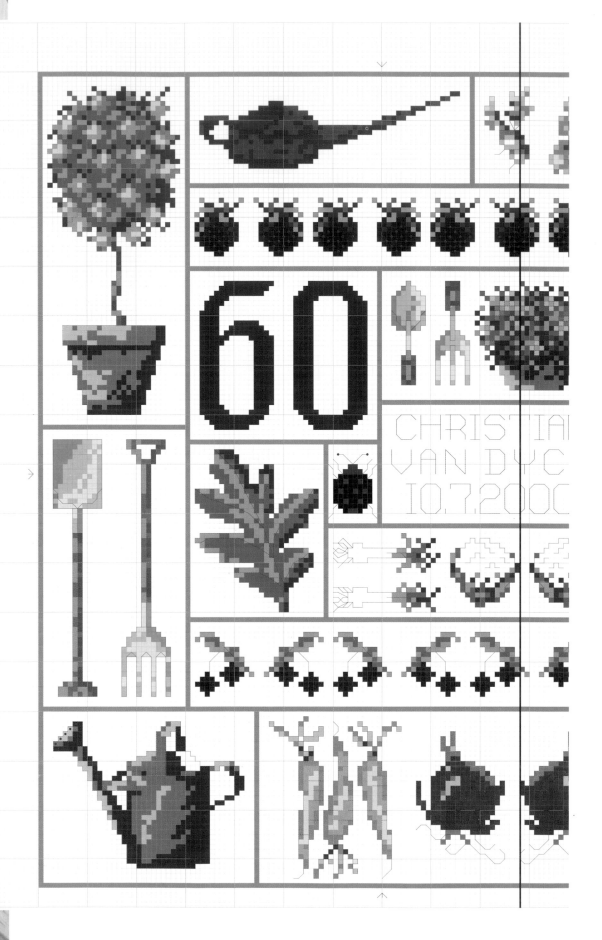

## METHOD

**1** To prevent the fabric edges from fraying, neaten by either taping with masking tape or hemming.

**2** Locate the centre of the fabric by folding in half horizontally and vertically. You may find it easier to mark the fold lines by tacking with a contrasting thread. Use a hoop or frame to help keep the tension even and the fabric taut (see page 123).

**3** Locate the centre of the design using the arrows at the edge of the chart. Begin at the centre of the design with your first cross stitch and continue working outwards.

**4** Backstitch the letters and numbers using two strands of thread. Elsewhere, stitch using two strands of thread for cross stitch and one strand for backstitch. Use two strands of thread for the french knots (see page 125). For the alphabet see page 116.

## MAKING UP

**1** When the design is complete, remove the hoop or frame and press. If necessary, wash the fabric prior to pressing it.

**2** Stretch the fabric to ensure that it is taut and frame. Alternatively, take your sampler along to an experienced picture framer.

KEY TO CHART  ● = French knot

# Jewellery Box

*This attractive jewellery box would find a home on even the most elegant of dressing tables. The shimmering colours of glass perfume bottles are beautifully captured by this design.*

## MATERIALS

- 1 piece of 27ct blue Aida
12 in x 10 in (30 cm x 25 cm)

- Medium size trinket box, 7½ in x 6 in
(19 cm x 15.5 cm), with a removable
cover that is adaptable for tapestry or
cross stitch

- 1 skein of each of the following
colours of thread:

DMC blanc

DMC 603 pink

DMC 602 mid pink

DMC 601 deep pink

DMC 5284 gold metallic/729
mid gold (1 strand of each)

DMC 869 dark old gold

DMC 3765 very dark aquamarine

DMC 598 turquoise

DMC 597 mid turquoise

DMC 3811 very light turquoise

DMC 798 mid blue

DMC 797 mid royal blue

DMC 796 very dark royal blue

DMC 333 dark purple

DMC 3746 purple

DMC 340 mid lilac

## METHOD

**1** To prevent the fabric edges from fraying, neaten by either taping with masking tape or hemming.

**2** Locate the centre of the fabric by folding in half horizontally and vertically. You may find it easier to mark the fold lines by tacking with a contrasting thread. Use a hoop or frame to help keep the tension even and the fabric taut (see page 123).

**3** Locate the centre of the design using the arrows at the edge of the chart. Begin at the centre of the design with your first cross stitch and continue working outwards.

**4** Stitch using two strands of thread for cross stitch. Use two strands of DMC 869 for backstitching the lettering. Use one strand of thread for the remaining backstitch. Backstitch the outline and detail of the tall bottle using DMC 796, the purple bottle using DMC 333, the aqua bottle using DMC 3765 and the label on the purple bottle using DMC 869. Use DMC 601 to backstitch the outline of the pink bottle and use DMC 869 for the outline of the gold cap. Backstitch the outline and detail of the lipstick cases using DMC 869 and the outline of the lipstick using DMC 601.

## MAKING UP

**1** When the design is complete, remove the hoop or frame and press. If necessary, wash the fabric prior to pressing it.

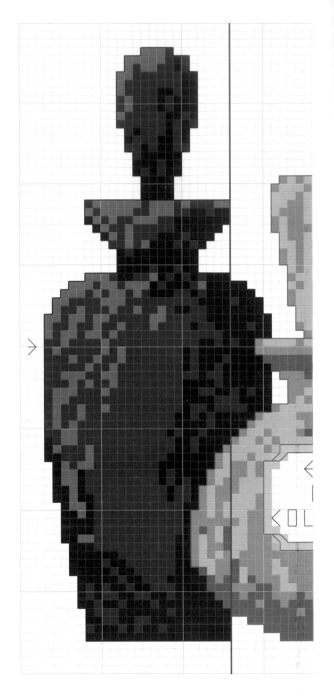

**2** Attach the embroidery to the removable cover, following the box manufacturer's instructions. Take care to ensure that the fabric is taut and that there are no wrinkles or creases once it has been attached.

# Sports Theme Birthday Card

*From fishing fanatics to golfing enthusiasts, this birthday card has something for everyone and will prove popular with sports addicts of all ages.*

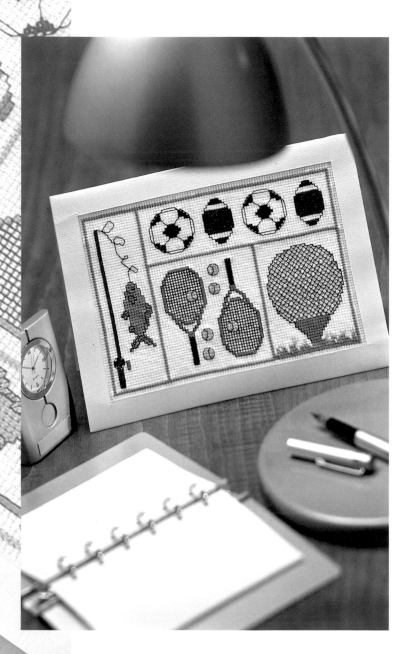

## MATERIALS

- 1 piece of 14ct white Aida 12 in x 10 in (30.5 cm x 25 cm)

- 1 white greetings card blank with rectangular opening measuring 7 in x 5 in (17.5 cm x 12.5 cm)

- Double-sided adhesive tape

- 1 skein of each of the following colours of thread:

  DMC 307 lemon yellow

  DMC 498 deep red

  DMC 902 red/brown

  DMC 988 mid green

  DMC 989 light green

  DMC 826 blue

  DMC 310 black

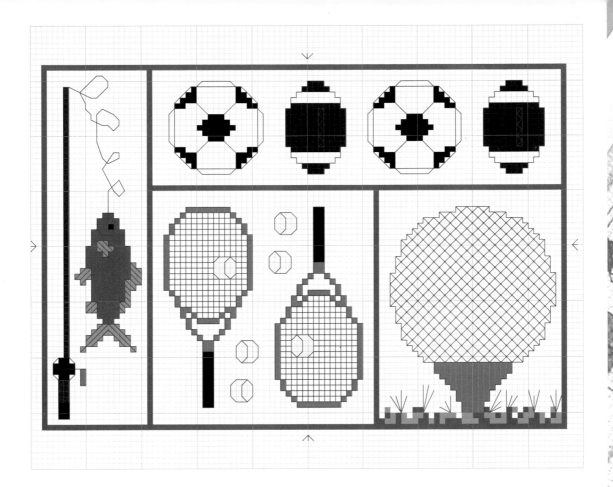

## METHOD

**1** To prevent the fabric edges from fraying, neaten by either taping with masking tape or hemming.

**2** Locate the centre of the fabric by folding in half horizontally and vertically. You may find it easier to mark the folds by tacking with a contrasting thread. Use a hoop or frame to help keep the tension even and the fabric taut (see page 123).

**3** Locate the centre of the design using the arrows at the edge of the chart. Begin at the centre of the design with your first cross stitch and continue working outwards.

**4** Stitch using two strands of thread for cross stitch. Backstitch the outlines and detail of the sports equipment and fish using one strand of DMC 310 and backstitch the blades of grass using one strand of DMC 988.

## MAKING UP

**1** When the design is complete, remove the hoop or frame and press. If necessary, wash the fabric prior to pressing it.

**2** Apply double-sided adhesive tape to the inside of the card around the edges of the opening. Position the embroidery to ensure that the design appears in the centre of the opening and stick down.

**3** Looking at the inside of the card, place double-sided adhesive tape around the inside of the bottom flap and fold the card over to cover the back of the embroidery.

# Floral Birthday Card

*Floral motifs are always popular for birthday cards and suit all ages. Here, an embroidered bunch of flowers tied together with a delicate bow is the centrepiece.*

## METHOD

**1** To prevent the fabric edges from fraying, neaten by either taping with masking tape or hemming.

**2** Locate the centre of the fabric by folding in half horizontally and vertically. You may find it easier to mark the fold lines by tacking with a contrasting thread. Use a hoop or frame to help keep the tension even and the fabric taut (see page 123).

**3** Locate the centre of the design using the arrows at the edge of the chart. Begin at the centre of the design with your first cross stitch and continue working outwards.

**4** Cross stitch using two strands of thread and backstitch the flower stems with two strands of DMC 700.

## MAKING UP

**1** When the design is complete, remove the hoop or frame and press. Wash the fabric prior to pressing it if necessary.

**2** Attach the ribbon to the flower stems with one cross stitch and tie into a bow.

**3** Using a craft knife, cut out 8 or 9 small leaf shapes around the edge of the front of the card. Carefully glue around the edges of the leaf shapes on the inside of the greetings card and stick small pieces of ribbon over the openings.

**4** Apply double-sided adhesive tape to the inside of the card around the edges of the opening. Carefully position the embroidery to ensure that the design appears in the centre of the opening and stick down.

**5** Looking at the inside of the card, place double-sided adhesive tape around the inside of the left-hand flap and fold the card over to cover the back of the embroidery.

### MATERIALS

• 1 piece of 14ct cream Aida
8 in x 6 in (20 cm x 15 cm)

• 10 in (25 cm) of narrow apricot ribbon

• 6 in (15 cm) of ribbon in a contrasting colour, or a selection of contrasting colours, 1 in (2.5 cm) wide

• 1 cream greetings card blank with rectangular opening measuring 3¾ in x 5¾ in (9.5 cm x 14.5 cm)

• Double-sided adhesive tape

• Fabric glue

• 1 skein of each of the following colours of thread:

DMC 5270 red metallic

DMC 3328 mid red

DMC 5279 rust metallic

DMC 721 mid orange

DMC 722 light orange

DMC 3825 apricot

DMC 743 mid yellow

DMC 704 light leaf green

DMC 702 mid leaf green

DMC 5269 green metallic

DMC 800 light sky blue

DMC 809 mid sky blue

DMC 5291 blue metallic

DMC 5289 purple metallic

# Christenings

# Christening Photograph Frame

*This charming frame is an ideal christening gift. Its classic design will appeal to young and old, ensuring its place as a treasured family heirloom.*

## MATERIALS

- 1 piece of 14ct oatmeal Aida 13 in x 14 in (33 cm x 36 cm)

- 1 piece of medium-weight iron-on interfacing 13 in x 14 in (33 cm x 36 cm)

- Wadding (batting) 8⅓ in x 10 in (21.5 cm x 25 cm)

- 2 pieces of white mount board 8⅓ in x 10 in (21.5 cm x 25 cm), one with 4 in x 6 in (10 cm x 15 cm) window cut out of the centre, one for the backing

- White fabric to cover backing 9½ in x 21 in (24 cm x 53.5 cm)

- Strut cut from mount board 3 in x 6 in (7.5 cm x 15 cm)

- Picture glass 5 in x 7 in (12.5 cm x 18 cm) optional

- Adhesive tape

- 1 skein of each of the following colours of thread:

  DMC 225 very light rose

  DMC 778 light rose

  DMC 5288 pink metallic

  DMC 3726 very dark rose

## METHOD

**1** To prevent the fabric edges from fraying, neaten by either taping with masking tape or hemming.

**2** Locate the centre of the fabric by folding in half horizontally and vertically. You may find it easier to mark the fold lines by tacking with a contrasting thread. Use a hoop or frame to help keep the tension even and the fabric taut (see page 123).

**3** Locate the centre of the design using the arrows at the edge of the chart and count out from this point to the top of the border. Count out the same distance from the centre of the Aida and begin stitching here.

**4** Stitch using two strands of thread for cross stitch, one strand of thread for backstitch and two strands of thread for french knots (see page 125). Please note that the broken pink line around the inside of the design shows the edge of the frame and is for reference only.

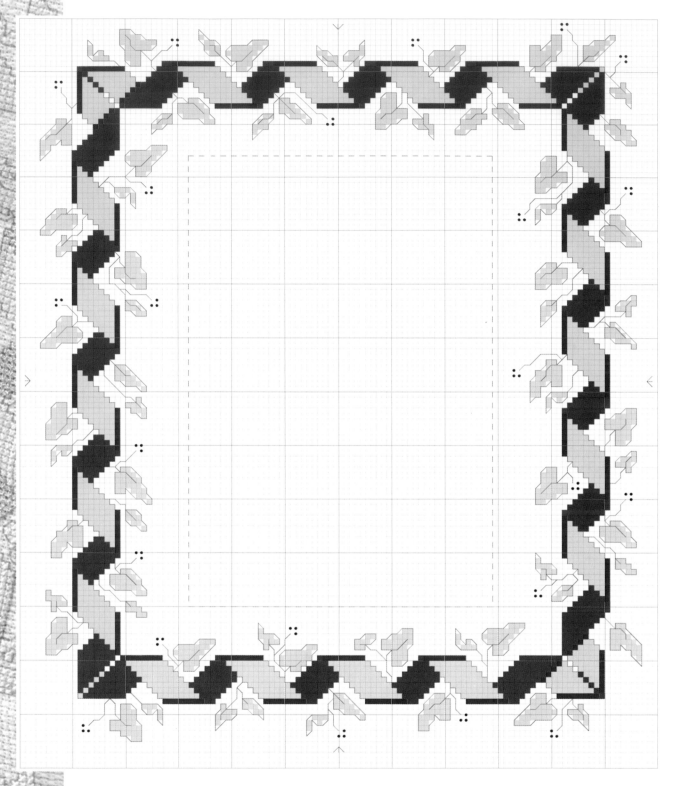

KEY TO CHART  • = French knot

## MAKING UP

**1** When the design is complete, remove the hoop or frame and press. If necessary, wash the fabric prior to pressing it.

**2** Attach the iron-on interfacing to the reverse of your embroidery, following the manufacturer's instructions.

**3** Assemble the front of the frame by putting the wadding on top of the piece of mount board with an opening. Carefully place the embroidery right side up on top of the wadding, ensuring that it is placed centrally so that the design frames the opening but does not overlap it.

**4** Fold the outside edge of the Aida over to the back of the mount board and check that the design and the fabric are straight. Pin the excess Aida to the edge of the mount board to hold it in place.

**5** Turn the frame over to look at the back of the board and use sharp scissors to carefully cut through the Aida from the centre of the opening into each corner.

**6** Push the flaps through to the back of the frame and cut the excess fabric to a width of 1 in (2.5 cm) all round. Pin the flaps to the back of the mount board ensuring that the opening is square and neat.

**7** Lace the outside edges of the Aida and the flaps folded back from the opening together over the back of the frame using button hole thread. Check to ensure that the corners of the opening are mitred and that the design and fabric grain are straight. Pull the thread tightly as you lace to remove any wrinkles in the fabric.

**8** If you wish to use glass, attach it firmly to the back of the photo frame using strong adhesive tape.

**9** Cover the second piece of mount board with the white fabric. Fold the fabric over the edges of the board, ensuring that the fabric covering the backing board is taut. Turn in the edges and stitch the edges together using ladder stitch.

**10** Place the frame and the backing board wrong sides together. Ladder stitch along the top of three edges, leaving the bottom edge open for inserting the photographs.

**11** Attach the strut to the backing board with strong adhesive tape.

# Butterfly Shawl

*What could be more beautiful than embroidered butterflies flying across a blue woollen shawl? This christening shawl is so attractive that it is guaranteed to become a family favourite.*

## MATERIALS

- 1 piece of blue lightweight wool fabric 1 yd x 1 yd (1 m x 1 m)

- 1 piece of fleece 1 yd x 1 yd (1m x 1m)

- 4¼ yd (4.25 m) of blue ribbon 2 in (5 cm) wide

- 1 piece of 11ct Aida to use as waste canvas – allow 6 in x 6 in (15 cm x 15 cm) for each butterfly you wish to embroider

- 1 skein of each of the following colours of thread:

  DMC 3689 pale candy pink

  DMC 3688 mid pink

  DMC 3687 raspberry pink

  DMC 3803 aubergine

  DMC 794 sky blue

  DMC 793 lilac

  DMC 3807 mid lilac

  DMC 792 dark lilac

## METHOD

**1** Decide how many butterflies you would like to appear on your shawl. You can embroider as many as you want, choosing from the selection of designs on pages 50–51.

**2** Tack 6 in x 6 in (15 cm x 15 cm) of 11ct Aida to the shawl where you want to position a butterfly. Use a hoop or frame to help keep the tension even and the fabric taut (see page 123).

**3** Locate the centre of your chosen butterfly design. Begin at the centre of the design with your first cross stitch and work outwards.

**4** Use three strands of thread to cross stitch through the Aida and the fabric. Do not do the backstitch yet. When the cross stitch has been completed, carefully remove the Aida one strand at a time (see page 122).

**5** Once the waste canvas has been removed, backstitch using two strands of thread.

**6** Repeat until you have embroidered all the butterflies.

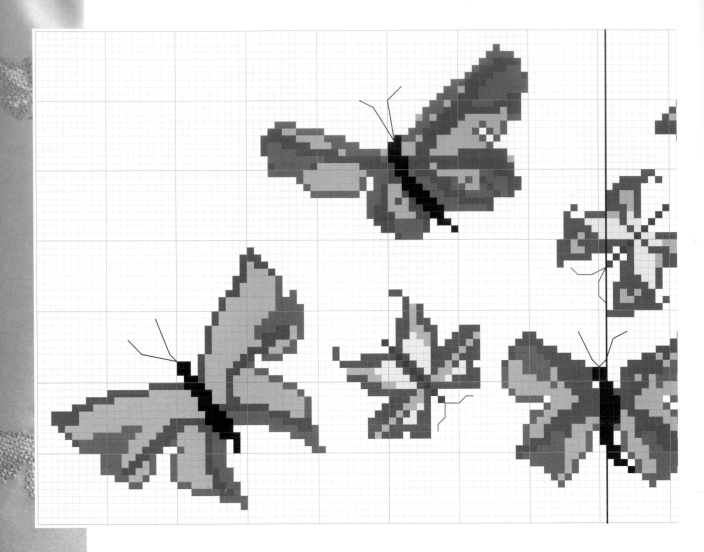

## MAKING UP

**1** When you have finished the embroidery, remove the hoop or frame and press.

**2** Ensure that the fleece is the same size as the wool fabric and lay the fleece over the back of the embroidery.

**3** Iron the ribbon in half and carefully pin into position around the edge of the shawl, ensuring that all the edges of the wool and fleece are under the ribbon.

**4** Fasten the ribbon to the wool and fleece by machine stitching around the outside edge of the shawl.

**5** If the shawl has become dirty, wash according to the manufacturer's instructions and press.

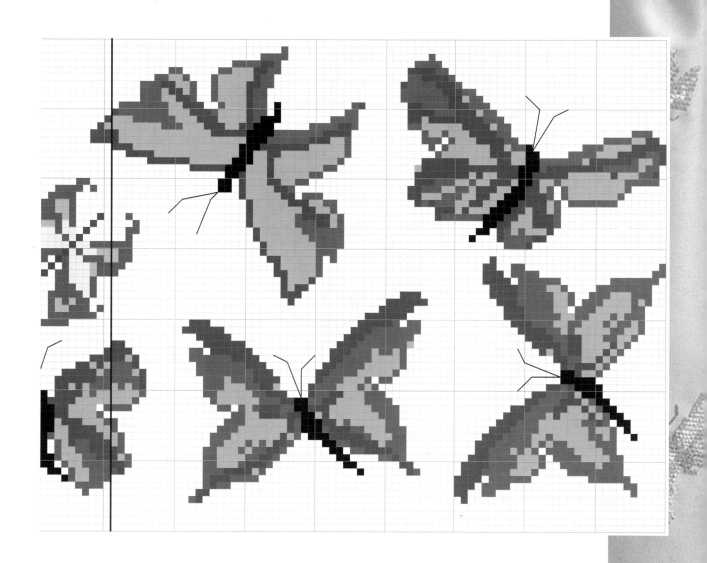

# Christening Gown

*Decorating your child's christening gown with delicate rosebuds will ensure that the gown looks fantastic. Further embroidery could be added to a cap or bootees to create a perfectly accessorized outfit.*

## MATERIALS

- 1 christening gown

- 1 piece of 18ct Aida to use as waste canvas – allow 2 in x 2 in (5 cm x 5 cm) for each rose motif you wish to embroider

- 1 skein of each of the following colours of thread:

  ☐ DMC blanc

  ▧ DMC 842 mocha brown

## METHOD

**1** Decide where you would like to position the rose motifs.

**2** Tack 2 in x 2 in (5 cm x 5 cm) of 18ct Aida to the gown where you want to position a rose. Use a hoop or frame to help keep the tension even and the fabric taut (see page 123).

**3** Locate the centre of the design using the arrows at the edge of the chart. Begin at the centre of the design with your first cross stitch and continue working outwards.

**4** Use two strands of thread to cross stitch through the Aida and the fabric.

**5** When the cross stitch has been completed, carefully remove the Aida one strand at a time (see page 122).

**6** Repeat until you have embroidered all the roses.

## MAKING UP

**1** When you have finished the embroidery, remove the hoop or frame and press. If necessary, wash the gown prior to pressing it.

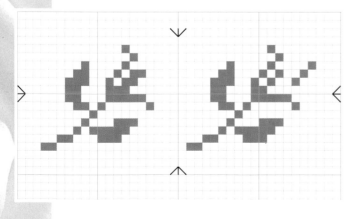

# Photograph Album Cover

*Create a personal record of a special day with this pretty album cover. It will make the perfect home for all the photographs and mementos from the christening day.*

### MATERIALS

- 1 photo album

- 1 piece of 18ct antique white Aida. You will need to allow enough material to cut out 1 piece to pattern A (see Method), adding at least 1 in (2.5 cm) to each side, and 2 pieces to pattern B (see Method)

- 1 piece of lining fabric, the same size as pattern A

- Wadding (batting), the same size as pattern A

- 1 piece of iron-on interfacing, the same size as pattern A

- 1 yd (1 m) of pink ribbon

- 1 pack of pearl beads

- 1 skein of each of the following colours of thread:

  DMC ecru
  DMC 754 flesh
  DMC 818 pale shell pink

  DMC 3354 mid candy pink
  DMC 3731 dark pink
  DMC 3778 mid rose brown
  DMC 841 mid mocha brown
  DMC 729 mid gold
  DMC 543 light beige brown
  DMC 677 straw
  DMC 992 dark mint green
  DMC 993 mid mint green
  DMC 598 turquoise
  DMC 747 very light turquoise
  DMC 809 mid sky blue
  DMC 798 mid blue
  DMC 211 very light lilac
  DMC 341 light lilac
  DMC 340 mid lilac
  DMC 310 black

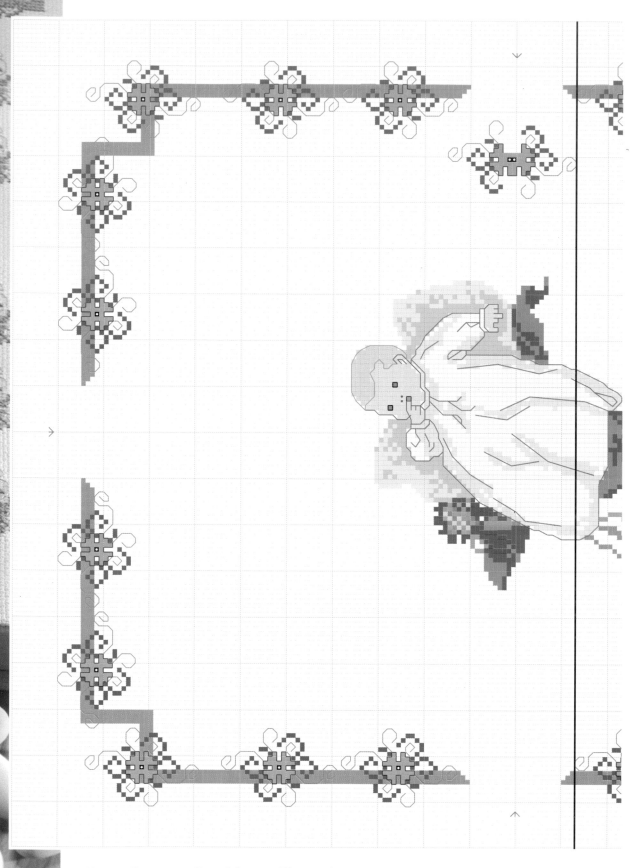

KEY TO CHART  • = French knot  ◻ = Bead

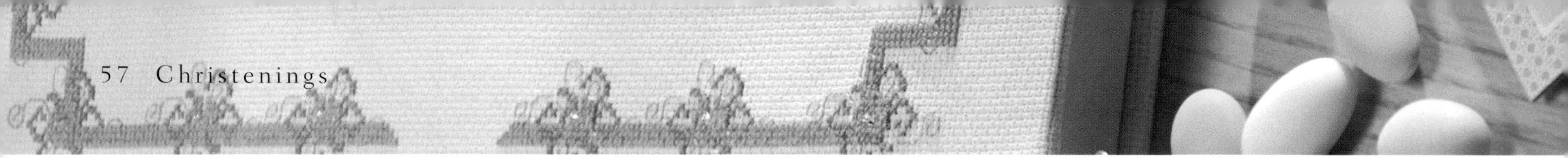

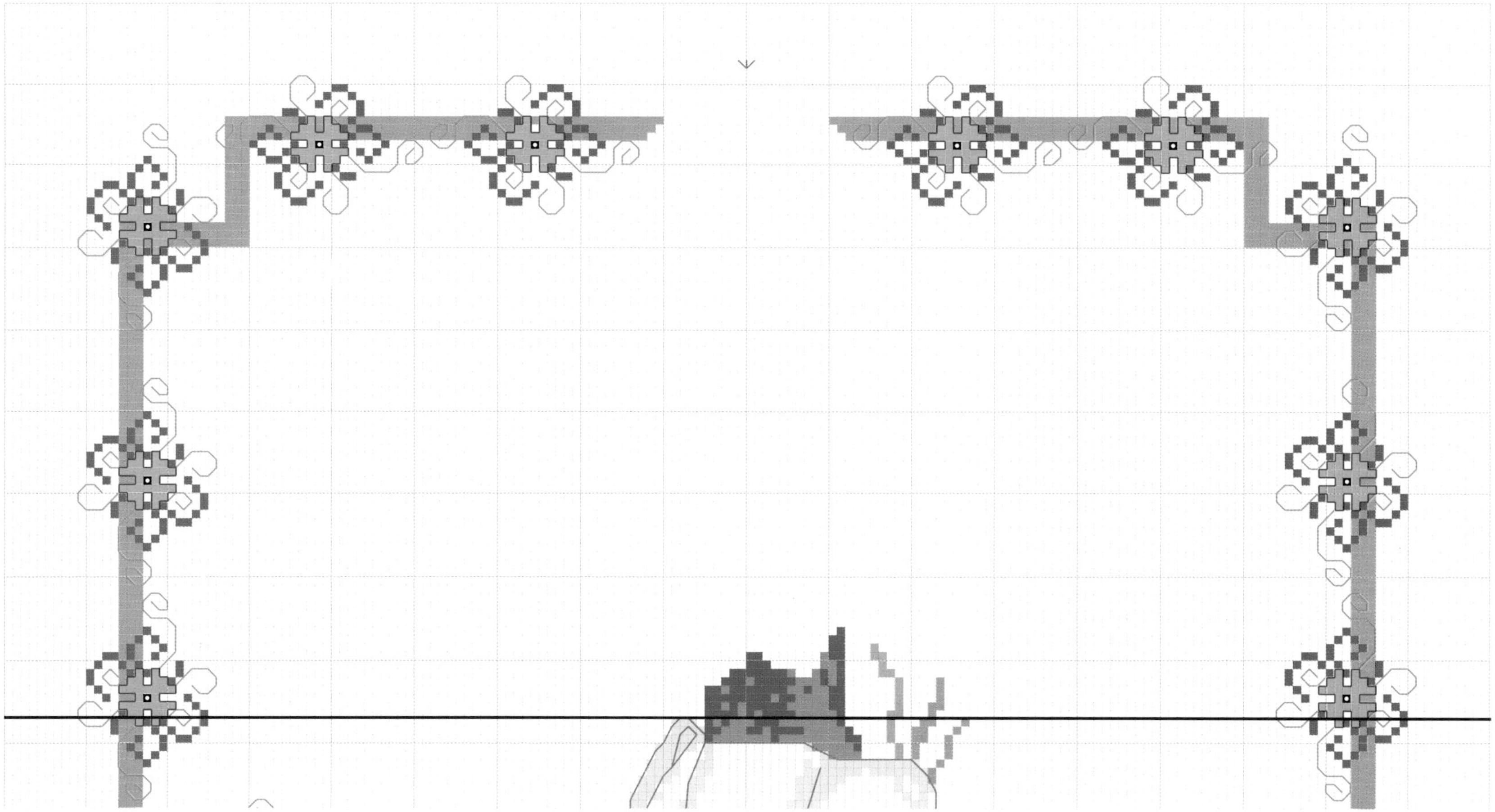

## METHOD

**1** Measure the height and width (back cover + spine + front cover) of your chosen photo album. Transfer these measurements to graph paper and then add ⅜ in (1 cm) to each measurement as a seam allowance. Mark this as pattern A.

**2** Mark the exact position of the album spine on pattern A. Your pattern should now be divided into a front cover, spine and back cover, with a seam allowance around the edge. Using a ruler, mark the centre of the front cover on pattern A.

**3** Measure the height of the album cover and three quarters of the width of the inside cover. Transfer these measurements to graph paper and then add ⅜ in (1 cm) to each measurement as a seam allowance. Mark this as pattern B.

**4** Pin pattern A onto the Aida and mark out the pattern. Add an extra 1 in (2.5 cm) beyond the marked edges and carefully cut out the material.

**5** Using pattern A, mark the centre of the front cover onto the Aida. You may find it easier to mark the centre by tacking with a contrasting thread. Remove the pattern from the Aida.

**6** To prevent the fabric edges from fraying, neaten by either taping with masking tape or hemming.

**7** Start at the point where you have marked the centre of the front cover. Use a hoop or frame to help keep the tension even and the fabric taut (see page 123).

**8** Locate the centre of the design using the arrows at the edge of the chart. Begin at the centre of the design with your first cross stitch and continue working the stitches outwards.

**9** Stitch using two strands of thread for cross stitch and two strands of thread for the french knots (see page 125). Use one strand of thread for all the backstitch. Backstitch the outline of the hair using DMC 729, the face and hands using DMC 3778 and the eyes using DMC 798. Backstitch the outline and detail of the gown with DMC 841, the outline of the pink flowers with DMC 3731 and the detail of the greenery with DMC 993.

## MAKING UP

**1** When the design is complete, remove the hoop or frame and press. If necessary, wash the fabric prior to pressing it.

**2** Mark out and cut the lining fabric, wadding and iron-on interfacing to the same size as pattern A.

**3** Mark out and cut two pieces of Aida to pattern B. These will become the inside flaps of the album cover.

**4** Position the inside flaps, right side up in front of you. Ensure that the sides of the fabric that are the same height as the album are to your left and right. Turn the right edge of each flap under by ¼ in (5 mm) and machine stitch the hem.

**5** Place the wadding on top of the wrong side of the embroidery and tack the two materials together along the outside edge.

**6** Following the manufacturer's instructions, attach the iron-on interfacing to the wrong side of the lining fabric.

**7** Cut the pink ribbon in half. Turn one end of half the ribbon under by ¾ in (2 cm) and position, fold side down, to front of the album cover, where the flower to the right of the child is indented. Tack the ribbon securely in place. Repeat with the second length of ribbon, attaching it to the centre of the edge of the back cover.

**8** Place the embroidery right side up. Arrange the two inside flaps right side down on top of the embroidery at each edge, so that their hemmed edges point towards the spine. Place the lining fabric right side down on top of the embroidery and inside flaps. Pin all the materials firmly together.

**9** Machine stitch around the edges, allowing ¼ in (5 mm) seam allowance, and leave an opening in the short edge of what will be the back cover. Be careful not to catch the ribbons in the stitching.

**10** Trim the excess material at the corners and turn the photo album cover right sides out. Slip stitch the opening you left in the edge of the back cover.

**11** Carefully press the album cover, ensuring that the embroidery is not flattened, and insert the photo album.

# Cake Band

*This wonderful beaded cake band will provide the ultimate finishing touch to a christening cake. Its simple and stylish design make this a really rewarding project to undertake.*

## MATERIALS

- 1 14ct white Aida band 3 in (7.5 cm) wide and as long as your cake requires

- 1 pack of cream seed beads

- Adhesive tape

- 1 skein of each of the following colours of thread:

  ☐ DMC ecru

  ▨ DMC 92 apple green variegated

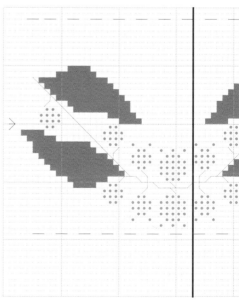

## METHOD

**1** Locate the centre of the fabric by folding in half horizontally and vertically. You may find it easier to mark the fold lines by tacking with a contrasting thread. Use a hoop or frame to help keep the tension even and the fabric taut (see page 123).

**2** Locate the centre of the design using the arrows at the edge of the chart. Begin at the centre of the design with your first cross stitch and continue working outwards. Please note that the broken black line around the design shows the edge of the cake band and is for reference only.

**3** Stitch using two strands of thread for cross stitch and backstitch. When using variegated thread, work each cross stitch separately rather than working in rows.

**4** Use one strand of DMC ecru thread to attach the cream seed beads with a half cross stitch.

**5** Repeat the pattern until the embroidery is as long as required.

## MAKING UP

**1** When the design is complete, remove the hoop or frame and press. If necessary, wash the fabric prior to pressing it.

**2** Wrap the embroidered band around the cake and fix in place at the back of the cake using adhesive tape.

KEY TO CHART   • = Bead

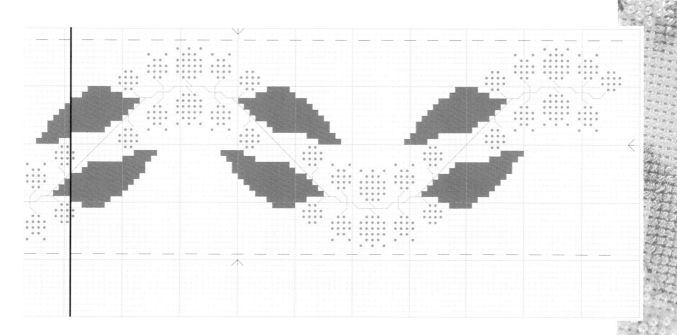

# Christening Sampler

*Reminiscent of a church window, the beautiful colours and rich embroidery make this sampler an exceptionally attractive wall hanging.*

## MATERIALS

- 1 piece of 14ct white Aida 12 in x 17 in (31 cm x 44 cm)
- 1 skein of each of the following colours of thread:

  DMC ecru

  DMC 353 flesh

  DMC 962 mid pink

  DMC 3773 mid pink/beige

  DMC 352 apricot

  DMC 676 light gold

  DMC 729 mid gold

  DMC 3829 dark gold

  DMC 3814 dark jade green

  DMC 991 very dark jade green

  DMC 823 navy*

  DMC 794 sky blue

  DMC 793 lilac

  DMC 792 dark lilac

* Please note that DMC 823 appears as black on the chart.

## METHOD

**1** To prevent the fabric edges from fraying, neaten by either taping with masking tape or hemming.

**2** Locate the centre of the fabric by folding in half horizontally and vertically. You may find it easier to mark the fold lines by tacking with a contrasting thread. Use a hoop or frame to help keep the tension even and the fabric taut (see page 123).

**3** Locate the centre of the design using the arrows at the edge of the chart. Begin at the centre of the design with your first cross stitch and continue working outwards.

**4** Stitch using two strands of thread for cross stitch and two strands of thread for the french knots (see page 125). Use DMC 991 to backstitch the flower stems. Use one strand of DMC 823 to backstitch around the eyes, noses and the outlines and details of the flowers. Use one strand of DMC 3773 to outline and detail the babies' bodies. Backstitch the lettering, numbering and the outlines and details of the hair using two strands of DMC 3829. (You will find a chart for a complete alphabet on page 121.)

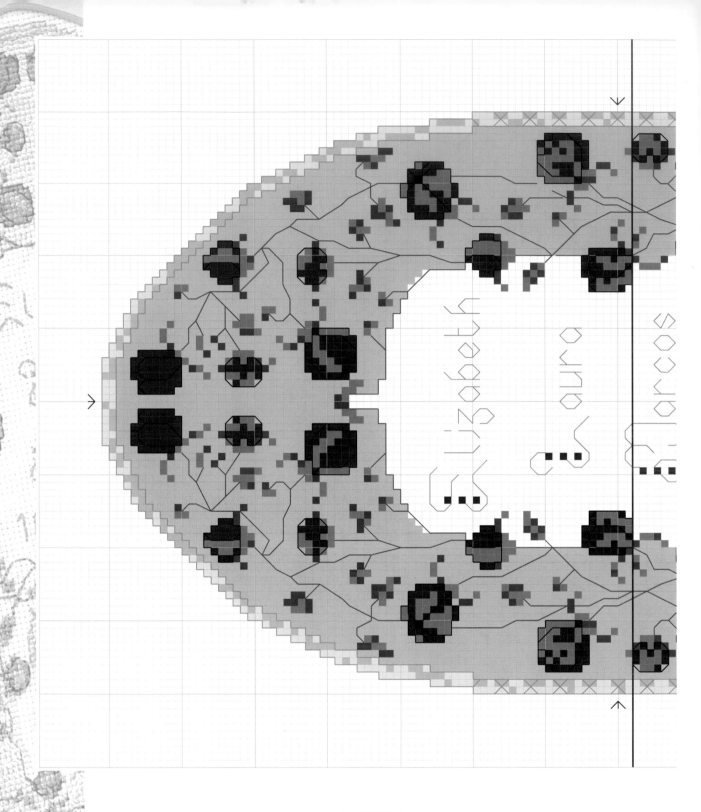

## MAKING UP

**1** When the design is complete, remove the hoop or frame and press. If necessary, wash the fabric prior to pressing it.

**2** Stretch the fabric to ensure that it is taut and frame. Alternatively, take your sampler along to an experienced picture framer.

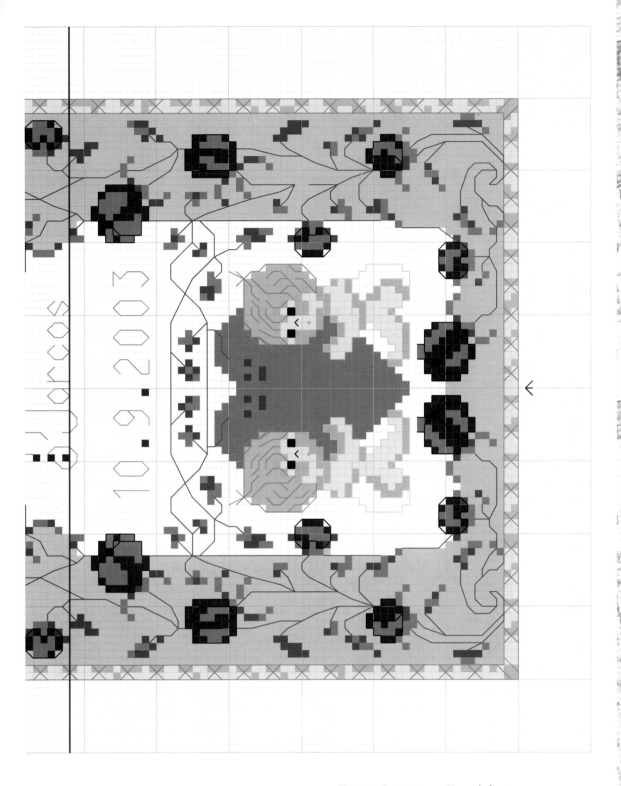

KEY TO CHART   ● = French knot

# Engagements
# & Weddings

# Engagement Card

*Embellished with luxurious gold embroidery and delicate beading, this cross stitch engagement ring is an excellent choice for making a very special card.*

## MATERIALS

- 1 piece of 14ct white Aida 6 in x 6 in (15 cm x 15 cm)

- 1 parchment greetings card blank with a round opening measuring 3½ in (9 cm) in diameter

- ½ yd (50 cm) of blue ribbon ½ in (1.5 cm) wide

- 1 box of mirror beads

- Double-sided adhesive tape

- 4 small star sequins

- 1 skein of each of the following colours of thread:

|  |  |
|---|---|
| ☐ | DMC blanc |
| ▨ | DMC 5284 gold metallic/ DMC 729 mid gold (1 strand of each) |
| ▨ | DMC 829 dark gold |
| ▨ | DMC 826 blue |
| ▨ | DMC 825 dark blue |
| ▨ | DMC 823 navy |

## METHOD

**1** To prevent the fabric edges from fraying, neaten by either taping with masking tape or hemming.

**2** Locate the centre of the fabric by folding in half horizontally and vertically. You may find it easier to mark the fold lines by tacking with a contrasting thread. Use a hoop or frame to help keep the tension even and the fabric taut (see page 123).

**3** Locate the centre of the design using the arrows at the edge of the chart. Begin at the centre of the design with your first cross stitch and continue working outwards.

**4** Stitch using two strands of thread for cross stitch. Combine one strand of DMC 729 and one strand of DMC gold metallic to form two strands of thread for the gold cross stitch.

**5** Backstitch the detail around the sapphire using two strands of DMC 823 and the outline of the gold using one strand of DMC 829. Use two strands of DMC 729 to backstitch the lettering.

**6** Use one strand of DMC blanc to attach the beads with a half cross stitch.

## MAKING UP

**1** When the design is complete, remove the hoop or frame and press. If necessary, wash the fabric prior to pressing it.

**2** Apply double-sided adhesive tape to the inside of the card around the opening. Carefully position the embroidery to ensure that the design appears in the centre of the opening and stick down.

**3** Looking at the inside of the card, place double-sided adhesive tape around the inside of the left-hand flap and fold the card over to cover the back of the embroidery.

**4** Using a craft knife, carefully make two parallel cuts, ½ in (1.5 cm) long, at the top of the card's fold and thread the ribbon through it.

**5** Decide where you would like to position your star sequins and glue them to the front of the card.

KEY TO CHART ◙ = Bead

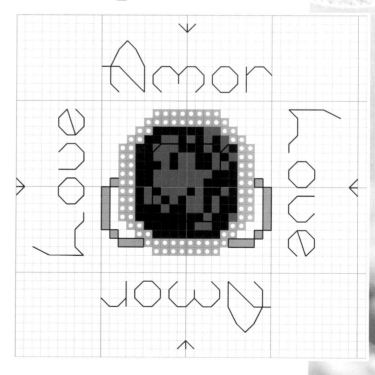

# Wedding Cake Card

*A wedding is one of the most important occasions in a person's life, so why not mark the day by making a hand-made card? This lovely embroidered wedding cake will certainly be a hit with the happy couple.*

## MATERIALS

- 1 piece of 18ct snow-blue Aida 8 in x 6 in (20 cm x 15 cm)

- 1 white greetings card blank with oval opening measuring 4½ in x 3 in (11.5 cm x 7.5 cm)

- Double-sided adhesive tape

- 1 skein of each of the following colours of thread:

| | |
|---|---|
| | DMC ecru |
| | DMC 818 pale shell pink |
| | DMC 3354 mid candy pink |
| | DMC 676 light gold |
| | DMC 729 mid gold |
| | DMC 472 light pea green |
| | DMC 471 mid pea green |
| | DMC 597 mid turquoise |
| | DMC 598 turquoise |
| | DMC 341 light lilac |
| | DMC 340 mid lilac |
| | DMC 415 light silver grey |
| | DMC 414 dark silver grey |

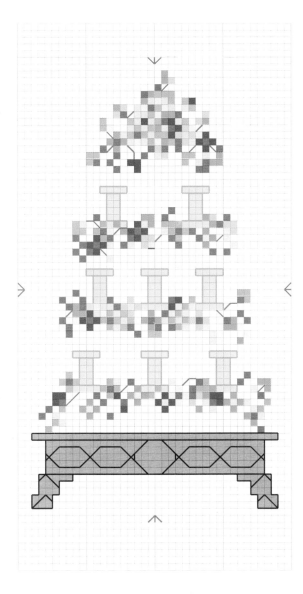

hoop or frame to help keep the tension even and the fabric taut (see page 123).

**3** Locate the centre of the design using the arrows at the edge of the chart. Begin at the centre of the design with your first cross stitch and continue working outwards.

**4** Use two strands of thread for cross stitch. Backstitch the outline of the columns using one strand of DMC 729, the pattern of the cake stand using one strand of DMC 414 and the flower stems using one strand of DMC 471.

## MAKING UP

**1** When the design is complete, remove the hoop or frame and press. If necessary, wash the fabric prior to pressing it.

**2** Stick double-sided adhesive tape to the inside of the card around the opening. Carefully position the embroidery to ensure that the design appears in the centre of the opening and stick down.

**3** Looking at the inside of the card, place double-sided adhesive tape around the inside of the left-hand flap and fold the card over to cover the back of the embroidery.

## METHOD

**1** To prevent the fabric edges from fraying, neaten by either taping with masking tape or hemming.

**2** Locate the centre of the fabric by folding in half horizontally and vertically. You may find it easier to mark the fold lines by tacking with a contrasting thread. Use a

# Wedding Bouquet Sampler

*Finished with gold lettering, seed beads and pink ribbon, this cross stitch wedding bouquet is a sumptuous gift to celebrate the start of a couple's life together.*

## MATERIALS

- 1 piece of 14ct white Aida 12 in x 19 in (30.5 cm x 48.5 cm)
- 1 yd (1 m) of pink ribbon ¼ in (5 mm) wide
- 1 large box of pink seed beads
- 1 skein of each of the following colours of threads:

DMC blanc

DMC 3354 mid candy pink

DMC 3733 mid pink

DMC 3731 dark pink

DMC 3350 magenta

DMC 680 gold

DMC 729 mid gold

DMC 989 light green

DMC 988 mid green

DMC 987 dark green

DMC 809 mid sky blue

DMC 799 deep sky blue

## METHOD

**1** To prevent the fabric edges from fraying, neaten with masking tape or hem.

**2** Locate the centre of the fabric by folding in half horizontally and vertically. You may find it easier to mark the fold lines by tacking with a contrasting thread. Use a hoop or frame to help keep the tension even and the fabric taut.

**3** Locate the centre of the design using the arrows at the edge of the chart. Begin at the centre of the design with your first cross stitch and continue working outwards.

**4** Cross stitch using two strands of thread. Backstitch the outline of the flowers with one strand of DMC 3350, the flower stems with one strand of DMC 987 and the letters and numbers using two strands of DMC 680. (You will find a chart for a complete alphabet on pages 118–19.)

**5** Use one strand of DMC 3733 to attach the seed beads with a half cross stitch.

**6** Place the ribbon on the outside edge of the embroidery, as shown in the chart, and carefully couch (see page 126) as indicated.

**7** Cut the ends of the ribbon to angles.

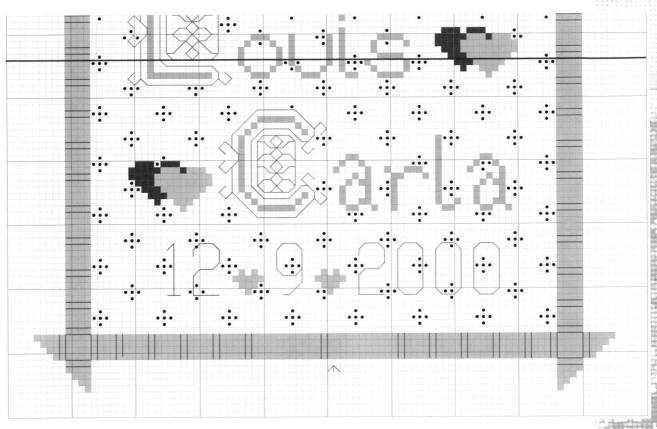

KEY TO CHART   • = Bead

## MAKING UP

**1** When the design is complete, remove the
hoop or frame and press. If necessary, wash
the fabric prior to pressing it.

**2** Stretch the fabric to ensure that it is taut
and frame. Alternatively, take your sampler to
an experienced picture framer.

# Scented Wedding Shoe Cushion

*Embroider a stylish cushion filled with fragrant herbs. This scented gift will bring back memories of a wedding long after the happy day.*

## MATERIALS

- 1 piece of 14ct ivory Aida 16 in x 10 in (41 cm x 26 cm)

- 2 pieces of ivory fabric 16 in x 7 in (41 cm x 17.5 cm)

- 2 pieces of ivory fabric 16 in x 3 in (41 cm x 7.5 cm)

- 2 pieces of ivory fabric 10 in x 3 in (26 cm x 7.5 cm)

- 1 piece of medium weight iron-on interfacing 16 in x 10 in (41 cm x 26 cm)

- 1 scented cushion pad 12 in x 7 in (30 cm x 17.5 cm)

- 1 box of ecru beads

- 1 skein of each of the following colours of thread:

  ☐ DMC ecru

  ☐ DMC 543 light beige brown

  ☐ DMC 842 mocha brown

  ☐ DMC 841 mid mocha brown

  ☐ DMC 597 mid turquoise

  ☐ DMC 598 turquoise

  ☐ DMC 3810 dark turquoise

  ☐ DMC 3809 very dark turquoise

## METHOD

**1** To prevent the fabric edges from fraying, neaten by either taping with masking tape or hemming.

**2** Locate the centre of the fabric by folding the material in half horizontally and vertically. You may find it easier to mark the fold lines by tacking with a contrasting thread. Use a hoop or frame to help keep the tension even and the fabric taut (see page 123).

**3** Locate the centre of the design using the arrows at the edge of the chart. Begin at the centre of the design with your first cross stitch and continue working outwards.

**4** Cross stitch using two strands of thread. Backstitch the outline and detail of the shoe with one strand of DMC 841 and use one strand of DMC 3809 to backstitch the outline and detail of the bow. Backstitch the stems and the lettering with two strands of DMC 3809. (You will find a chart for a complete alphabet on page 120.)

**5** Attach the beads with a half cross stitch using one strand of DMC ecru.

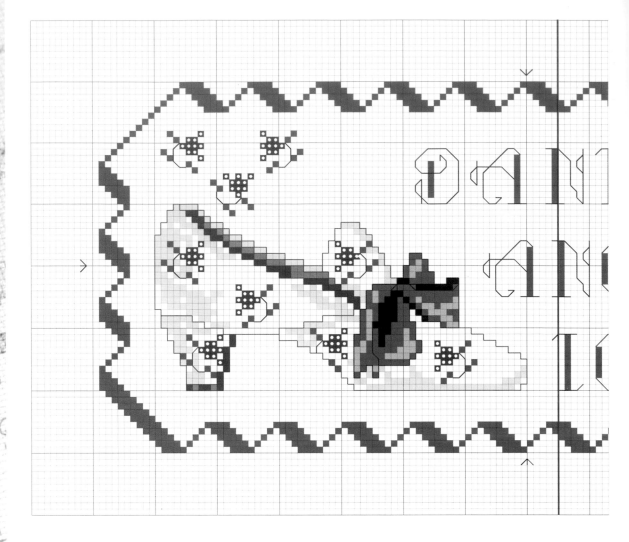

## MAKING UP

**1** When the design is complete, remove the hoop or frame and press. If necessary, wash the fabric prior to pressing it.

**2** Take the four narrow pieces of ivory fabric and machine stitch a ⅔ in (1 cm) hem along one long edge on each piece. These strips will eventually frame the design and form the front of the cushion.

**3** Place the frame strips right sides down, hemmed edges towards the middle, to form a window 10½ in x 5 in (26.5 cm x 13 cm). Where the strips meet, fold back the edges diagonally to form mitred corners and mark the diagonal fold with tailor's chalk on the wrong side of the fabric. Machine stitch the strips right sides together along the chalk line. Trim excess material.

**4** Attach the iron-on interfacing to the reverse of the embroidery, following the manufacturer's instructions.

**5** Place the ivory fabric frame right side up on top of the embroidery. Carefully position the frame to ensure that the design appears in the centre of the opening and pin the frame to the Aida. Machine stitch the materials together, stitching around the

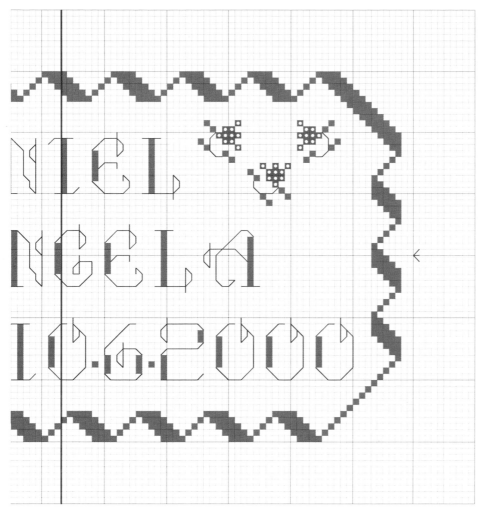

KEY TO CHART ▣ = Bead

inside edge of the frame and along the mitred edges to ensure that the ivory fabric is firmly attached to the Aida.

**6** Take the two large pieces of ivory fabric and machine stitch a 1 in (2.5 cm) hem along one long edge on each piece. These two pieces of fabric will eventually form the back of the cushion.

**7** Place the framed embroidery right side up and position the two pieces of hemmed fabric right sides down on top of the embroidery with the hemmed edges overlapping in the middle. Pin all the layers of fabric together.

**8** Allowing a 1 in (2.5 cm) seam, machine stitch around the outside edges of the Aida and ivory fabric. Trim the excess material at the corners and turn right side out.

**9** Insert a store-bought or hand-made scented cushion pad into the cushion cover. You can always refresh your scented cushion with a few drops of the appropriate essential oil when the fragrance begins to fade.

# Wedding Ring Cushion

*This delicate cushion will be a delightful addition to any wedding service, and can be kept for many years to come as a memento of the couple's special day.*

## MATERIALS

- 1 piece of 27ct antique white evenweave 12 in x 12 in (30.5 cm x 30.5 cm)

- 1 piece of ivory or cream fabric for backing 12 in x 12 in (30.5 cm x 30.5 cm)

- 1 piece of medium weight iron-on interfacing 12 in x 12 in (30.5 cm x 30.5 cm)

- 1 cushion pad 8 in x 8 in (20.5 cm x 20.5 cm)

- 1 yd (1 m) of ivory or cream cord

- 20 in (50 cm) of narrow ivory or cream ribbon

- 1 box of very small ecru beads

- 1 skein of each of the following colours of thread:

  - ☐ DMC ecru
  - ☐ DMC 738 very pale gold
  - ☐ DMC 437 mid gold
  - ☐ DMC 436 dark gold

## METHOD

**1** To prevent the fabric edges from fraying, neaten by either taping with masking tape or hemming.

**2** Locate the centre of the fabric by folding in half horizontally and vertically. You may find it easier to mark the fold lines by tacking with a contrasting thread. Use a hoop or frame to help keep the tension even and the fabric taut (see page 123).

**3** Locate the centre of the design using the arrows at the edge of the chart. Begin at the centre of the design with your first cross stitch and continue working outwards.

**4** Stitch using two strands of thread for cross stitch and two strands of thread for the backstitch.

**5** Attach beads with a half cross stitch.

**6** Stitch the initials, positioning them three squares from the hearts and two squares apart. (You will find a chart for a complete alphabet on page 120.)

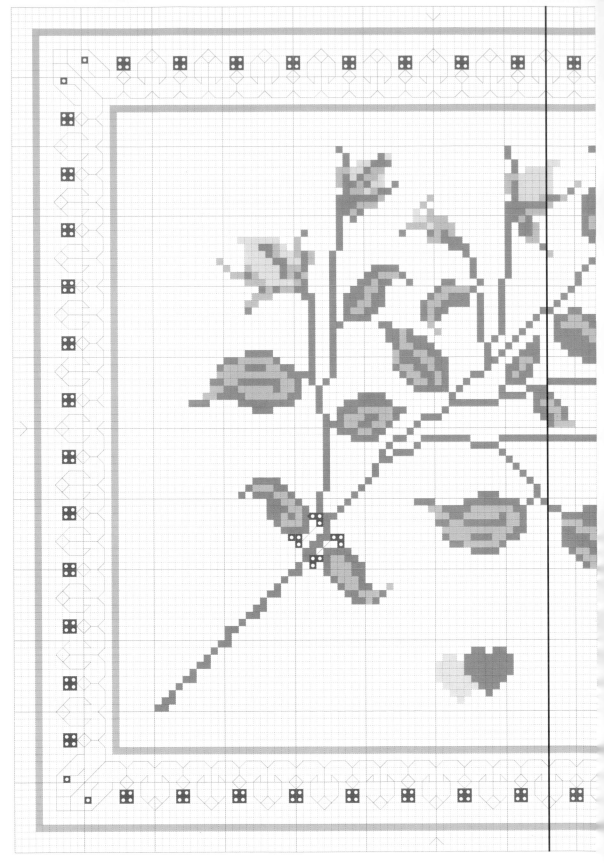

KEY TO CHART   ▣ = Bead

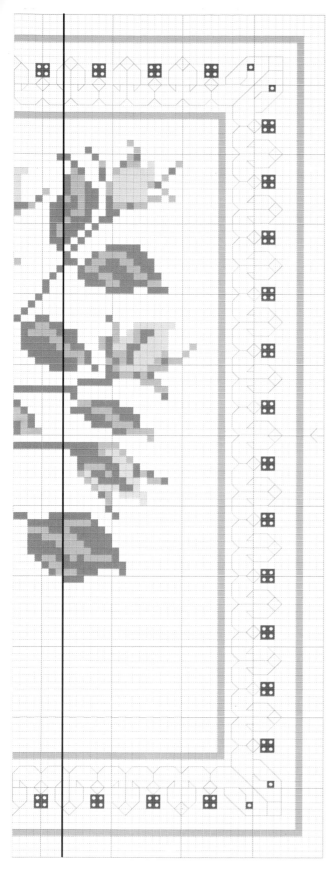

## MAKING UP

**1** When the design is complete, remove the hoop or frame and press. If necessary, wash the fabric prior to pressing it.

**2** Attach the iron-on interfacing to the reverse of the embroidery, following the manufacturer's instructions.

**3** Attach the ribbon to the front of the embroidery. Right sides together, machine stitch around the outside edge, being careful not to catch the embroidery or ribbon. Leave an opening so that the cushion pad may be inserted.

**4** Turn the cushion right side out and insert the cushion pad. Slip stitch (see page 126) the opening in the cushion closed.

**5** Using slip stitch, attach the cord to the outside edge of the cushion.

# Bridesmaid's Dress

*Decorate a bridesmaid's dress with one of these innovative floral motifs. The vibrant flowers with their delicate beading will be the perfect finishing touch for any outfit.*

MATERIALS

- 1 bridesmaid's dress

- 1 piece of 18ct Aida to use as waste canvas – allow 3 in x 3 in (7.5 cm x 7.5 cm) for each flower motif you wish to embroider

### POINSETTIA MOTIF

- 1 box of red seed beads

- 1 skein of each of the following colours of thread:

  ▪ DMC 3712 light red

  ▪ DMC 3328 mid red

  ▪ DMC 347 red

  ▪ DMC 988 mid green

### FUCHSIA MOTIF

- 1 box of pink seed beads

- 1 skein of each of the following colours of thread:

  ▪ DMC 326 burgundy

  ▪ DMC 988 mid green

  ▪ DMC 333 dark purple

## METHOD

**1** This method can be used on most fabrics on which counting threads would not be possible, but ensure before you start that the fabric of your dress will not show tacking marks.

**2** Decide on where you would like to position the floral motifs.

**3** Tack 3 in x 3 in (7.5 cm x 7.5 cm) of 18ct Aida to the dress where you want to position a motif and use a hoop or frame to help keep the tension even and the fabric taut (see pages 122–23).

**4** Locate the centre of the design using the arrows at the edge of the chart. Begin at the centre of the design with your first cross stitch and continue working outwards.

**5** Use two strands of thread to cross stitch through the Aida and the fabric. Do not attach the beads or do any backstitch yet.

**6** When the cross stitch has been completed carefully remove the Aida one strand at a time (see page 122).

**7** Once all the waste canvas has been removed, use one strand of DMC 347 to attach the red seed beads, or one strand of DMC 326 to attach the pink seed beads, with a half cross stitch.

**8** For the fuchsia design, backstitch using one strand of DMC 988.

**9** Repeat until you have embroidered all your flowers.

### MAKING UP

**1** When you have finished the embroidery, remove the hoop or frame and press. If necessary, wash the dress according to the manufacturer's instructions prior to pressing it.

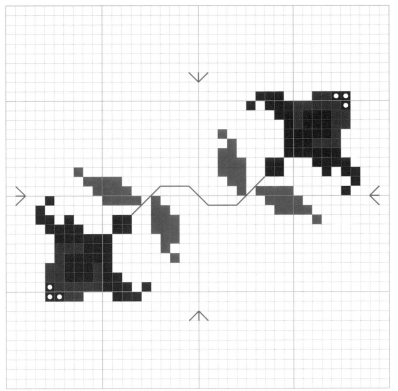

FUCHSIA

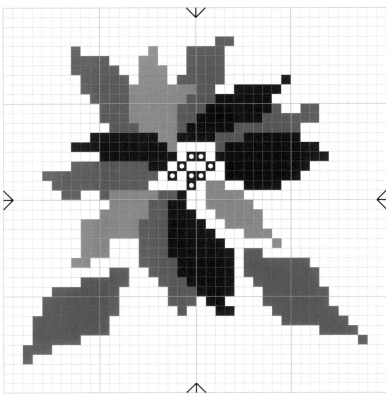

POINSETTIA

KEY TO CHART ◘ = Bead

# Drawstring Bag

*Accessorize a wedding or bridesmaid's dress with a pretty drawstring bag. This project is an easy way to add a personal touch to the wedding day. You could alter the colours so that they tone with the bride's bouquet.*

## MATERIALS

- 1 18ct white Aida band 22 in (56 cm) long and 1¾ in (4.5 cm) wide

- 1 piece of peach silk 20 in x 14 in (51 cm x 35.5 cm)

- 2 pieces of peach silk 8 in x 8 in (20.5 cm x 20.5 cm)

- 1 piece of cardboard 8 in x 8 in (20.5 cm x 20.5 cm)

- 1 yd (1 m) of ivory cord

- Cotton thread to match the silk

- 1 pack of seed pearls

- 1 skein of the following thread:

  DMC 754

## METHOD

**1** Locate the centre of the fabric by folding in half horizontally and vertically. You may find it easier to mark the fold lines by tacking with a contrasting thread. Use a hoop or frame to help keep the tension even and the fabric taut (see page 123).

**2** Locate the centre of the design using the arrows at the edge of the chart. Begin at the centre of the design with your first cross stitch and continue working outwards.

**3** Stitch using two strands of thread for cross stitch.

**4** Use one strand of thread to attach the seed pearls with a half cross stitch. Please note that in addition to the seed pearls indicated by the bead symbols on the chart, you need to attach pearls to the insides of the hearts. Within the hearts on the chart are a grid of lines, at each intersection of the lines attach a seed pearl.

**5** Repeat until the embroidery is as long as required to fit around the bag.

**1** When the design is complete, remove the hoop or frame and press. If necessary, wash the fabric prior to pressing it.

**2** Take the large piece of peach silk and make a ½ in (1.3 cm) hem on the two short sides and one long side.

**3** Turn over the long hemmed edge to the wrong side of the fabric by 2 in (5 cm). Pin the fold to the wrong side of the fabric and iron the fold flat. Machine stitch along this long edge, 1½ in (4 cm) from the ironed fold, to create a channel through which the drawstring cord will be threaded.

**4** Place the embroidered band on top of the right side of the large piece of peach silk. Carefully position the band 2 in (5 cm) from the unhemmed long edge of the fabric and pin in place. Machine stitch the band to the silk.

**5** Create a tube by folding the peach silk right sides together so that the two short ends of the fabric meet. Pin along the short edge and machine stitch a ½ in (1.3 cm) hem, being careful not to sew up the openings to the drawstring channel.

**6** Draw a circle with a radius of 3 in (7.5 cm) on the cardboard and cut around the drawn line. Using the cardboard template, mark the circle on the two squares of peach silk. Add an extra ½ in (1.3 cm) beyond the marked edges and cut out the material.

**7** Place the card circle between the two fabric circles. Ensure that it is in the centre and pin in place. Machine stitch around the marked circle so that the cardboard is stitched firmly between the two layers of fabric and there is a ½ in (1.3 cm) of material beyond the stitched edge.

**8** Insert the circular base into the unhemmed end of the tube so that raw edges meet. Hand-sew around the edge of the circle of card so that all the raw edges will be on the inside of the bag when it is turned right side out.

**9** Turn the tube right side out, so that the embroidered band runs around the outside edge of the bag.

**10** Thread the cord through the openings at the top of the bag. Knot the cord and fray the ends to create tassels.

KEY TO CHART  ● = Bead

# Wedding Photograph Frame

*Everyone will admire this handsomely embroidered gold and ecru photo frame. It is the perfect way to display a favourite wedding-day photograph.*

## MATERIALS

- 1 sheet of 14ct clear plastic canvas

- Photo frame with a rectangular opening 8 in x 6 in (20 cm x 15 cm)

- Glue (optional)

- 3 skeins of each of the following colours of thread:

  DMC ecru

  DMC 5284 gold metallic

## METHOD

**1** Locate the centre of the design using the arrows at the edge of the chart and count out from this point to the top of the border. Count out the same distance from the centre of the plastic canvas and begin stitching here.

**2** Cross stitch using three strands of DMC ecru. Long stitch using six strands of DMC gold metallic. Please note that the broken black line around the centre of the design is for reference only.

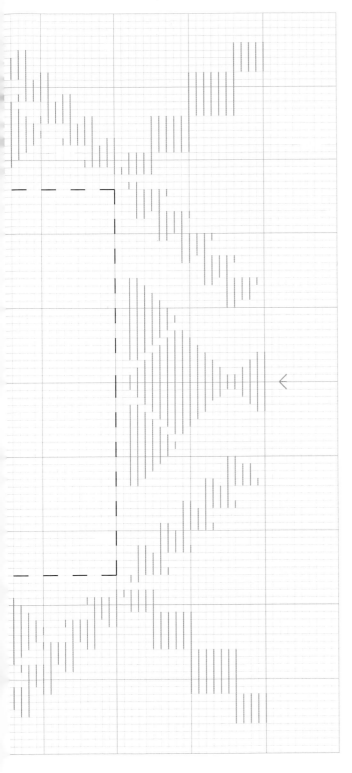

## MAKING UP

**1** Carefully cut around the inside and outside of the embroidery, leaving one row of plastic canvas from the edge of the stitching to the cut edge.

**2** Slip stitch (see page 126) around the inside edge of the frame to neaten the frame opening.

**3** Carefully glue the wrong side of the embroidery to the front of the photo frame, ensuring that the opening is clear and that the embroidery conceals the frame it is attached to. Alternatively, you could place the stitched frame underneath the glass of the photo frame.

# Anniversaries

# Silver Wedding Card

*A hand-made card brings a personal touch to any occasion. The opulent silver thread and beads make this a luxurious project that is fun to make, and even better to receive.*

## MATERIALS

- 1 piece of 14ct white Aida 8 in x 6in (20 cm x 15cm)

- 1 white greetings card blank with a rectangular opening 5½ in x 3½ in (14 cm x 9 cm)

- Double-sided adhesive tape

- 1 box of very small ecru beads

- 1 skein of each of the following colours of thread:

    DMC 3746 pale lilac
    DMC 5283 metallic silver

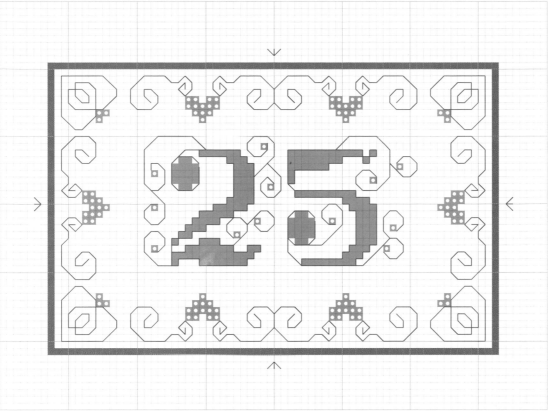

KEY TO CHART ◘ = Bead

## METHOD

**1** To prevent the fabric edges from fraying, neaten by either taping with masking tape or hemming.

**2** Locate the centre of the fabric by folding in half horizontally and vertically. You may find it easier to mark the fold lines by tacking with a contrasting thread. Use a hoop or frame to help keep the tension even and the fabric taut (see page 123).

**3** Locate the centre of the design using the arrows at the edge of the chart. Begin at the centre of the design with your first cross stitch and continue working outwards.

**4** Stitch using two strands of thread for cross stitch and two strands of thread for backstitch.

**5** Attach beads with a half cross stitch.

## MAKING UP

**1** When the design is complete, remove the hoop or frame and press. If necessary, wash the fabric prior to pressing it.

**2** Apply double-sided adhesive tape to the inside of the card around the edges of the opening. Carefully position the embroidery to ensure that the design appears in the centre of the opening and stick down.

**3** Looking at the inside of the card, place double-sided adhesive tape around the inside of the bottom flap and fold the card over to cover the back of the embroidery.

# Golden Wedding Sampler

*A golden wedding anniversary is an important family event. This exquisite sampler should be the perfect gift to celebrate 50 years of marriage.*

## MATERIALS

- 1 piece of 14ct ivory Aida
18 in x 18 in (46 cm x 46 cm)
- 1 skein of each of the following colours of thread:

DMC 738 very pale gold/pearl cotton no.5 straw

DMC 437 mid gold

DMC 5284 gold metallic

DMC 435 light brown

DMC 502 mid grey/green

DMC 501 dark grey/green

DMC 5289 purple metallic

DMC 550 very dark purple

DMC 552 dark purple

DMC 553 mid purple

DMC 554 light lilac

## METHOD

**1** To prevent the fabric edges from fraying, neaten by either taping with masking tape or hemming.

**2** Locate the centre of the fabric by folding in half horizontally and vertically. You may find it easier to mark the fold lines by tacking with a contrasting thread. Use a hoop or frame to help keep the tension even and the fabric taut (see page 123).

**3** Locate the centre of the design using the arrows at the edge of the chart. Begin at the centre of the design with your first cross stitch and continue working outwards.

**4** Stitch using two strands of thread for cross stitch. Backstitch the alphabet and capital letters using two strands of DMC 552 and the remainder of the lettering using two strands of DMC 435. (You will find a chart for a complete alphabet on page 117.)

**5** Long stitch the flower heads and hearts using one strand of pearl cotton 738.

## MAKING UP

**1** When the design is complete, remove the hoop or frame and press. If necessary, wash the fabric prior to pressing it.

**2** Stretch the fabric to ensure that it is taut and frame. Alternatively, take your sampler along to an experienced picture framer.

# Ruby Wedding Photograph Frame

*This handsome photo frame is an ideal gift for a 40th wedding anniversary. It would be just right for displaying a picture of the couple celebrating their ruby wedding.*

## MATERIALS

- 1 piece of 14ct oatmeal Aida 18 in x 17 in (46 cm x 43 cm)

- 1 piece of medium-weight iron-on interfacing 18 in x 17 in (46 cm x 43 cm)

- 1 piece of wadding (batting) 18 in x 17 in (46 cm x 43 cm)

- 2 pieces of white mount board 11½ in x 10 in (29 cm x 25.5 cm), one with a 6 in x 4½ in (15 cm x 11 cm) window cut out, one for backing

- White fabric to cover backing 12½ in x 22 in (31.5 cm x 56 cm)

- Strut cut from mount board 3 in x 6 in (7.5 cm x 15 cm)

- Picture glass 7 in x 5½ in (18 cm x 14 cm) optional

- Adhesive tape

- 1 box of black seed beads

- 1 skein of each of the following colours of thread:

| | | | |
|---|---|---|---|
| ■ DMC 347 red | | ■ DMC 988 mid green |
| ■ DMC 304 mid red | | ■ DMC 987 dark green |
| ■ DMC 498 deep red | | ■ DMC 553 mid purple |
| ■ DMC 814 burgundy | | ■ DMC 552 dark purple |
| ■ DMC 349 orange red | | ■ DMC 310 black |
| ■ DMC 989 light green | | |

## METHOD

**1** To prevent the fabric edges from fraying, neaten by either taping with masking tape or hemming.

**2** Locate the centre of the fabric by folding in half horizontally and vertically. You may find it easier to mark the fold lines by tacking with a contrasting thread. Use a hoop or frame to help keep the tension even and the fabric taut (see page 123).

**3** Locate the centre of the design using the arrows at the edge of the chart and count out from this point to the top of the border. Count out the same distance from the centre of the Aida and begin stitching here.

**4** Stitch using two strands of thread for cross stitch. Use two strands of DMC 814 to back-stitch the detail and outline of the flowers and to backstitch around the numbers. Use one strand of DMC 310 to attach the beads with a half cross stitch to the flower centres.

## MAKING UP

**1** When the design is complete, remove the hoop or frame and press. If necessary, wash the fabric prior to pressing it.

**2** Attach the iron-on interfacing to the reverse of your embroidery, following the manufacturer's instructions.

**3** Assemble the front of the frame by putting the wadding on top of the piece of mount board with an opening. Carefully place the embroidery right side up on top of the wadding, ensuring that it is placed centrally so that the design frames the opening but does not overlap it.

**4** Fold the edges of the Aida over to the back of the board and check that the design and fabric are straight. Pin the excess Aida to the edge of the board to hold it in place.

**5** Turn the frame over to look at the back of the opening and use sharp scissors to cut through the Aida from the centre of the opening into each corner. Pull the flaps through to the back of the frame and cut the excess fabric to a width of 1 in (2.5 cm). Pin the flaps to the back of the mount board ensuring that the opening is square and neat.

**6** Lace the outside edges of the Aida and the folded back flaps together over the back of the frame with button hole

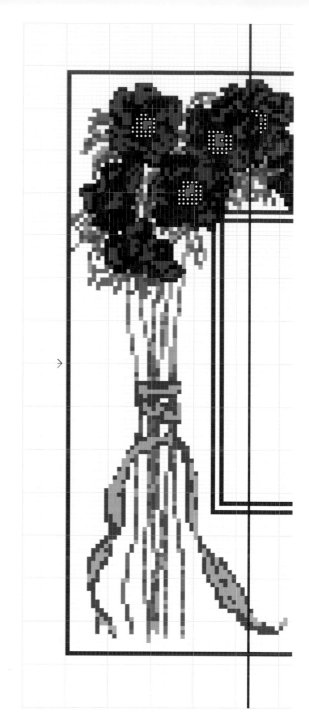

thread. Check to ensure that the corners of the opening are mitred and that the design and fabric grain are straight. Pull the thread tightly as you lace to remove any wrinkles in the fabric.

**7** If you wish to use glass, attach it to the back of the frame using strong adhesive tape.

**8** Cover the second piece of mount board with the white fabric. Fold the fabric over the edges of the board, ensuring that the fabric is taut. Turn in the edges and stitch the edges together using ladder stitch.

**9** Place the frame and the backing board wrong sides together. Ladder stitch along

KEY TO CHART ◻ = Bead

top of the three edges. Remember to leave the bottom edge of the frame open for inserting the photographs.

**10** Attach the strut to the backing board with strong adhesive tape.

# Family Tree Sampler

*A hand-made sampler is a marvellous way to capture your family history for future generations. In this design the family names are displayed within hearts hanging in a tree.*

## MATERIALS

- 1 piece of 14ct oatmeal Aida 14 in x 15 in (36 cm x 38 cm)

- 1 skein of each of the following colours of thread:

  DMC 677 straw

  DMC 676 light gold

  DMC 3829 dark gold

  DMC 435 light brown

  DMC 434 mid brown

  DMC 433 dark brown

  DMC 472 light pea green

  DMC 471 mid pea green

  DMC 470 dark pea green

  DMC 937 dark olive green

## METHOD

**1** The design provides six hearts for children's names. If you do not require all six hearts, then embroider only as many hearts as you need.

**2** To prevent the fabric edges from fraying, neaten by either taping with masking tape or hemming.

**3** Locate the centre of the fabric by folding in half horizontally and vertically. You may find it easier to mark the fold lines by tacking with a contrasting thread. Use a hoop or frame to help keep the tension even and the fabric taut (see page 123).

**4** Locate the centre of the design using the arrows at the edge of the chart. Begin at the centre of the design with your first cross stitch and continue working outwards.

**5** Stitch using two strands of thread for cross stitch. Backstitch the names and dates using two strands of DMC 937 and use one strand of DMC 937 for the remaining backstitch. (You will find a chart for a complete alphabet on page 116.)

## MAKING UP

**1** When the design is complete, remove the hoop or frame and press. If necessary, wash the fabric prior to pressing it.

**2** Stretch the fabric to ensure that it is taut and frame. Alternatively, take your sampler along to an experienced picture framer.

# Anniversary Photograph Album Cover

*Why not make a wedding anniversary album and fill it
with pictures and mementos from the couple's life together?
This heart-shaped wreath of pink sweet peas would make
an ideal cover for the photo album.*

## MATERIALS

- 1 photo album

- 1 piece of 28ct oatmeal
evenweave 9 in x 9 in
(23 cm x 23 cm)

- 1 yd (1 m) of pink ribbon

- Fabric glue

- 1 skein of each of the
following colours of thread:

  DMC 605 candy pink/
  5288 pink metallic
  (1 strand of each)

  DMC 604 light pink/
  5288 pink metallic
  (1 strand of each)

  DMC 603 mid pink/
  5288 pink metallic
  (1 strand of each)

  DMC 601 deep pink

  DMC 987 dark green/
  5269 green metallic
  (1 strand of each)

  DMC 988 mid green/
  5269 green metallic
  (1 strand of each)

  DMC 989 light green

## METHOD

**1** To prevent the fabric edges from fraying,
neaten by either taping with masking tape
or hemming.

**2** Locate the centre of the fabric by folding
in half horizontally and vertically. You may
find it easier to mark the fold lines by
tacking with a contrasting thread. Use a
hoop or frame to help keep the tension even
and the fabric taut (see page 123).

**3** Locate the centre of the design using the
arrows at the edge of the chart. Begin at the
centre of the design with your first cross
stitch and continue working outwards.

**4** Cross stitch using two strands of thread.
Backstitch the outline and detail of the
flowers with one strand of DMC 601 and
backstitch the stems, tendrils and the outlines of the leaves with one strand of
DMC 987.

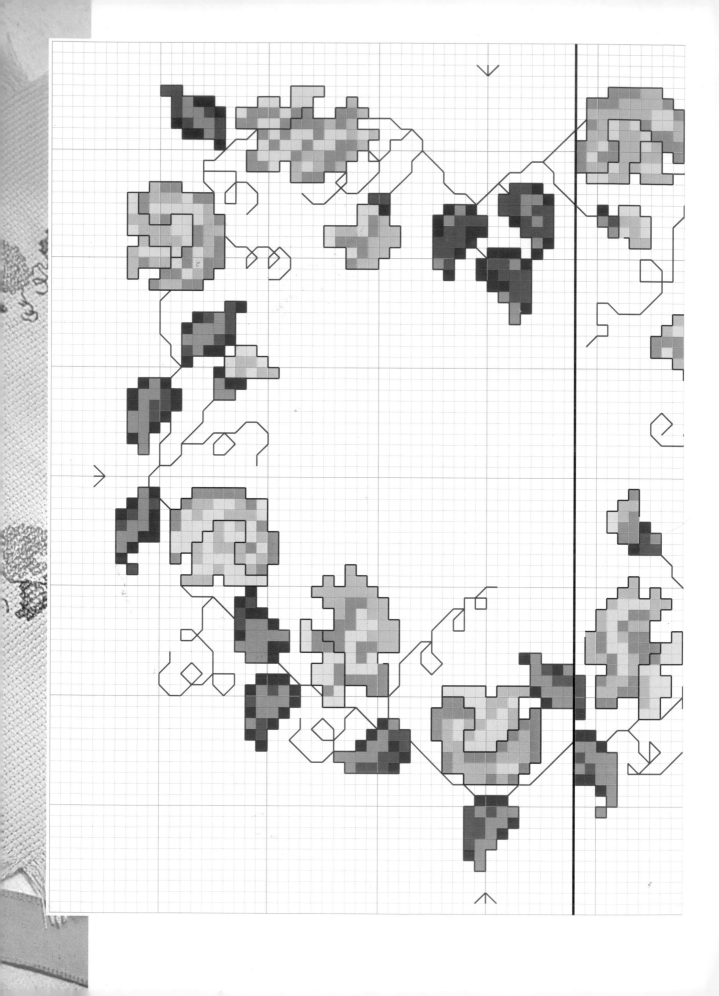

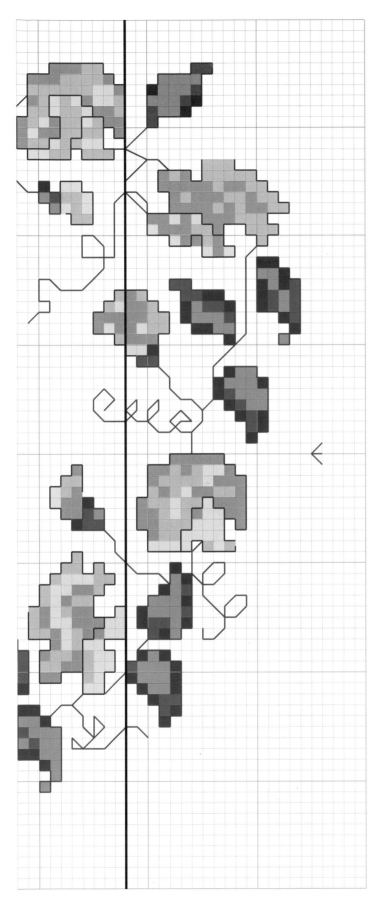

## MAKING UP

**1** When the design is complete, remove the hoop or frame and press. If necessary, wash the fabric prior to pressing it.

**2** Cut the fabric to a 7½ in x 7½ in (19.5 cm x 19.5 cm) square piece of material with the embroidery in the middle.

**3** Pull threads away from the edges of the fabric to create a fringe. Continue to remove threads until the material measures 6 in x 6 in (15 cm x 15 cm) and the fringe measures ¾ in (2 cm) long.

**4** Attach it to the front of your album with fabric glue.

**5** You can embellish the finished photograph album using the pink ribbon to match the embroidery.

# Alphabets and Templates

Whatever the occasion, embellishing your cross stitch with a name, a date, or even a message, is the perfect way to make a gift truly unique. To help you do this, you can use the alphabet charts on the following pages to personalize your work.

Each of these alphabets belongs to a particular project in the book, and is cross-referenced for easy use.

In addition, you may choose to use or adapt these alphabets for your own designs and projects.

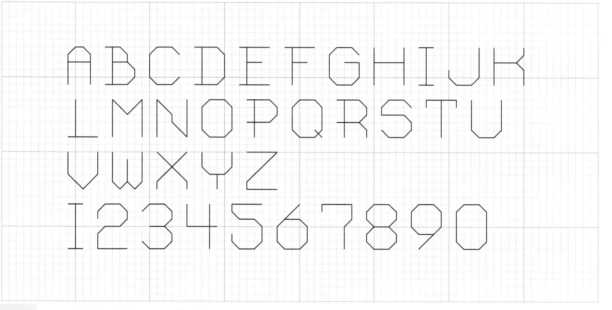

**60th Birthday Sampler** (page 30)

**Family Tree Sampler** (page 108)

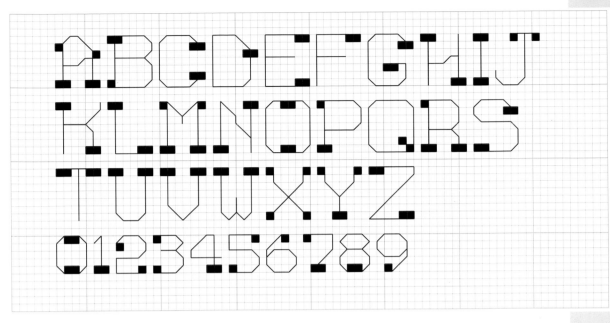

Animal Ark Sampler (page 16)

Golden Wedding Sampler (page 100)

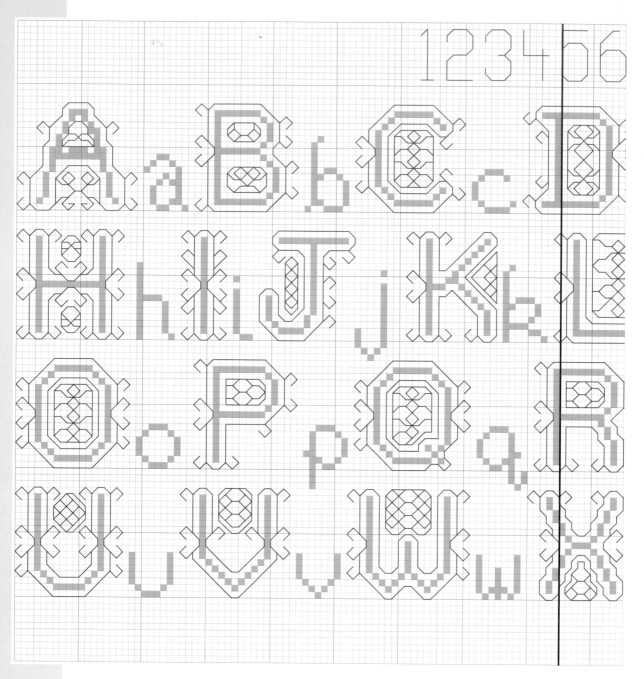

Wedding Bouquet Sampler (page 72)

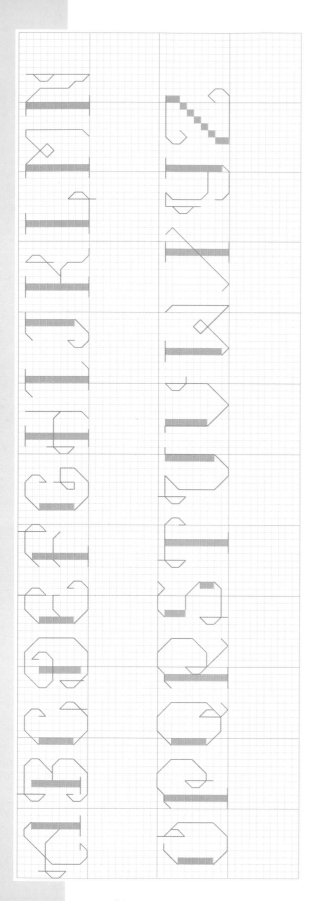

Wedding Ring Cushion (page 80)

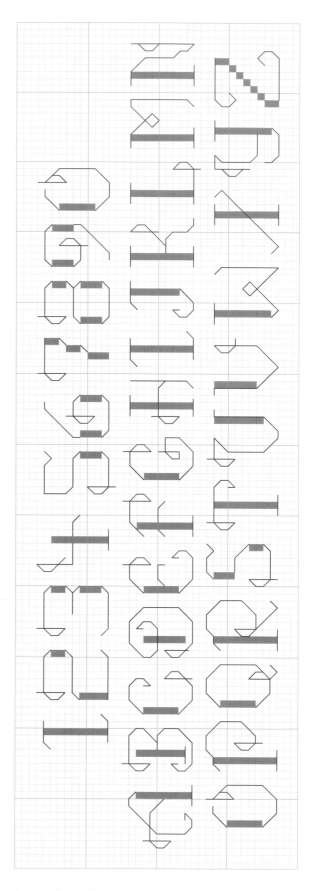

Scented Wedding Shoe Cushion (page 76)

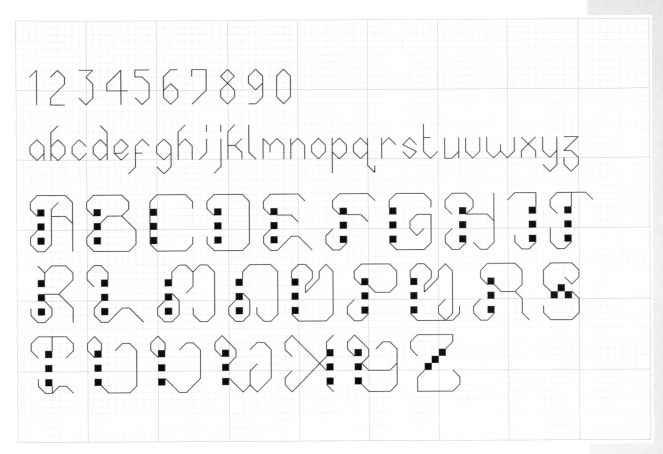

Christening Sampler (page 62)

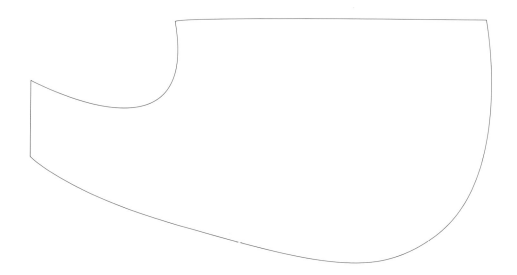

Bunny Rabbit Bib template (page 20)
*This template is for half the bib and is shown at 50% of the actual size. Photocopy this template, enlarging it by 200%, for the correct size.*

# Basic Materials and Techniques

## FABRICS

The projects in this book will generally require one of three types of fabric: Aida, evenweave or plastic canvas.

Aida is woven from blocks of threads and has a clear grid of holes. With Aida you simply work a single stitch per intersection, so it is an easy fabric for beginners to work on. It is available in a range of different counts (squares per inch) and you should select the appropriate count of fabric for your project.

Evenweave fabrics have an equal number of horizontal and vertical threads, and the count of an evenweave is determined by the number of threads per inch. Stitches are generally worked across 2 threads, but you could work your embroidery over a single thread, or a much larger number of them. This means, for example, that a 28ct evenweave stitched across two threads would be the same as a 14ct Aida.

Plastic canvas can be bought in A4 size sheets. It is more rigid than ordinary fabrics and is very easy to use. Plastic canvas can be bought in a wide range of colours and counts.

## HOW TO USE WASTE CANVAS

It is necessary to use waste canvas when you want to embroider a fabric that is not easy to count. Waste canvas comes in a variety of counts, and forms an instant grid to embroider across.

If you are working on a delicate or dry-clean fabric it is better to use Aida rather than a

### Using waste canvas

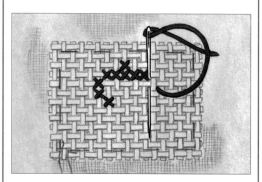

**1** *Simply tack the correct amount of canvas or Aida to your chosen fabric and sew through both layers of material. Only embroider the cross stitches before you remove the waste canvas, as the other stitches are more fragile and may be ruined.*

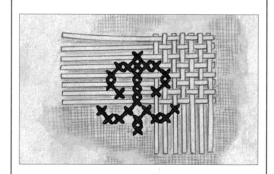

**2** *Once you have completed the cross stitch, carefully cut away the waste canvas around the stitching. When you have cut away as much as possible, begin to pull out the remaining threads, one thread at a time. If some of the threads prove a little difficult then remove using a pair of tweezers.*

regular waste canvas. This is because waste canvas needs to be made damp before it can be removed, so it is better to avoid it if you do not want to dampen the fabric you are working on. However, always check before you start stitching that the Aida will fray.

### HOW TO READ A CHART

The chart is quite simple to follow; one square on the chart represents one complete cross stitch and a straight line on the chart indicates backstitch. Each chart also has a key for special embellishments, such as french knots or beading. The charts are in colour, so match the colour on the chart to the colour key in the materials section to find out which DMC thread you need to use. To begin stitching, find the centre of the design by following the arrows at the edge of the chart and place your first stitch at the centre of your fabric. Always start from the centre and work outwards.

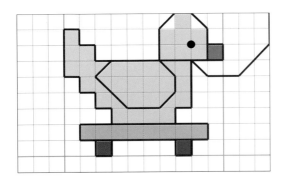

### SIZING UP OR SIZING DOWN A DESIGN

The materials list for each project specifies a count of fabric to use. However, it is easy to increase or decrease the size of the embroidered design by changing the count of your fabric. The higher the count (the more stitches per inch) the smaller the final design will be, and vice versa.

Do remember that you will need to amend the amounts of other materials you require in order to match the new size of the project. In particular, you may well need to use more thread if you increase the size of the design.

### USING A HOOP OR FRAME

Using a hoop or frame will keep the tension even and the fabric taut while you are working. An 8 in (20 cm) hoop is a good size, because it is easy to hold in one hand, but use a size that is appropriate to the size of the embroidery and always choose something that you find comfortable to work with.

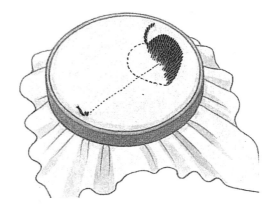

### WASHING AND PRESSING AN EMBROIDERED FABRIC

During the working of your design the fabric of your project may become soiled. If this happens, wash the embroidery in lukewarm water by hand but do not use biological washing powders. After rinsing, roll the embroidery in a towel and gently squeeze to remove as much water as possible. When the fabric remains only slightly damp, place the embroidery face down on top of a towel and iron on the reverse. It is important to do this in order to prevent the stitches from becoming flattened.

# EMBROIDERY STITCHES & SEWING TECHNIQUES

## CROSS STITCH

The basic cross stitch is formed by a diagonal cross worked between four corners of a square. The cross stitch is worked across an intersection on Aida fabric and over an even number of vertical and horizontal threads with evenweave cloth.

    The stitches can either be made one at a time, or worked in rows, so that a row of diagonal stitches is made in one direction and then they are all crossed by another diagonal row in the opposite direction. It is important to remember that the top diagonal stitches should always fall in the same direction in order to ensure an even finish to your embroidery.

    A half cross stitch is exactly what it sounds like. Very simply, it is one diagonal stitch that would be half of a cross stitch.

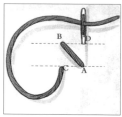

**Single cross stitch**
*Come up at A, down at B, up at C, down at D. You can reverse the stitch so that the top half slants from lower right to upper left.*

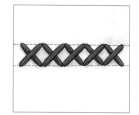

**1**  *To work a row, make even, equally spaced diagonal stitches, working from bottom to top. Then go down at top left of previous stitch to work back across the row.*

**2**  *Continue in the same manner, slanting stitches in the opposite direction to form a line of crosses.*

## ATTACHING BEADS WITH A HALF CROSS STITCH

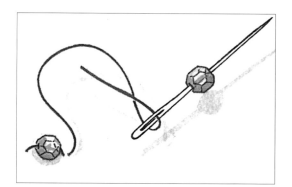

The easiest way to attach beads is to use a half cross stitch. Come up through the fabric, thread the bead onto the needle halfway through a diagonal stitch and go down through the fabric. It is advisable to stitch each bead twice to ensure that it is held firmly in place.

## LONG STITCH

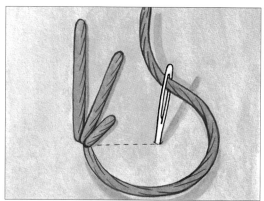

Long stitch is just a very long stitch that crosses more than one intersection or the standard number of threads. It can be used to add long straight lines to embroidered pictures.

## BACKSTITCH

Backstitch is a very simple stitch. The stitches should be small and even and they should resemble a neat row of stitches made on a sewing machine. Backstitch can be worked in straight lines or in curves and it is ideal for outlining or detailing in embroidery.

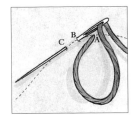

**1** *Working from right to left, come up at A, go down at B, then come up at C. Pull the thread through.*

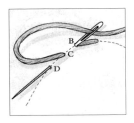

**2** *Go down again at B to make a backstitch, then come up at D, ready for the next stitch.*

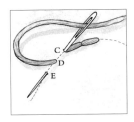

**3** *Pull the thread through, then go down at C and come up at E. Repeat as above to work a backstitched line.*

## FRENCH KNOTS

This versatile raised knot can be used either individually or in clusters to add interesting textures and shading to embroidery. The french knot technique is a little tricky, requiring practice, but it is certainly worth persevering.

**1** *Bring the needle up at A and wrap the thread around the needle once in a counter-clockwise direction.*

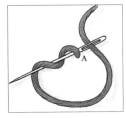

**2** *Wrap the thread around the needle a second time in the same direction, keeping the needle away from the fabric surface.*

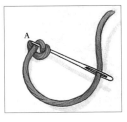

**3** *Push the wraps together and slide to the end of the needle. Go down close to the starting point and pull the thread through to form a knot.*

## BASTING

Basting is when you use large running stitches to hold two pieces of material together. You can also use basting to mark positions on a fabric.

**1** *Come up at A, go down at B, then come up at C. Do not pull the thread through the fabric.*

**2** *Go down at D and come up at E. Carefully pull the thread through so that the fabric does not pucker.*

**3** *Keeping your stitches even, repeat steps 1 and 2 until you have finished.*

## HEMMING

Hemming is used to neaten the edges of a fabric and to prevent it from fraying. It is important to hem the edges of your chosen fabric before you start to embroider to ensure that the material does not become frayed.

Before you start to work on your cross stitch project, either tape down the edges of the fabric with masking tape or stitch the hem in place. For most of the projects in this book it will be easiest to simply tape the hem.

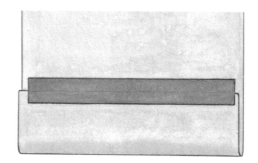

**Taping a hem**
To tape down the edges of the fabric, fold the fabric inwards and then secure it in place with masking tape.

**1** *Fold the fabric inwards and then fold it again to make three layers of fabric. Bring your needle up through the fold and pull the thread through.*

**2** *Go down just beneath the fold and then come up diagonally through the folded fabric. Repeat along the length of the fold, keeping the stitches even.*

**3** *Return across the row, working in the same way, but slanting your stitches in the opposite direction as above. Your stitches should form a neat row along the fold.*

## COUCHING

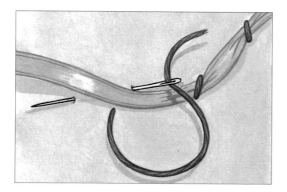

Couching is the method used for arranging thread or ribbon on a fabric and then stitching it in place with another thread. You can use a wide range of stitches when you are couching, from a simple stitch at right angles to the thread to more decorative stitches.

## SLIP STITCH

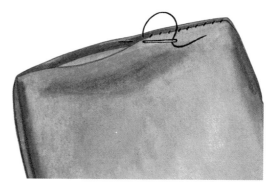

The almost invisible slip stitch is ideal for flat hemming or sewing pieces of material together. When using slip stitch it is important that the thread is not pulled taut and that the stitches are worked about ¼ in (5 mm) apart.

# Index

## A
Aida 122
alphabets 116–21
Animal Ark Sampler 16
anniversary projects 96–115
    Family Tree Sampler 108
    Golden Wedding Sampler 100
    Photograph Album Cover 112
    Ruby Wedding Photograph Frame 104
    Silver Wedding Card 98

## B
baby projects 8-–21
    Animal Ark Sampler 16
    Bunny Rabbit Bib 20
    New-born Baby Card 10
    Teddy Bear Shawl 12
    see also christening projects
backstitch 125
bag, drawstring 88
basting 125
beads, attaching 124
bib 20
Birthday Cup Cake Gift Tag 29
birthday projects 22–41
    Floral Birthday Card 40
    Gift Tags 26
    60th Birthday Sampler 30
    Sports Theme Birthday Card 38
    21st Birthday Card 24
Bridesmaid's Dress 84
Bumble Bee Gift Tag 28
Bunny Rabbit Bib 20
    template 121

## C
Cake Band 60
cards
    engagement 68
    floral birthday 40
    new-born baby 10
    silver wedding 98
    sports theme birthday 38
    21st birthday 24
    wedding cake 70
Champagne Bottle Gift Tag 29
charts, reading 123

christening projects 42–65
    Butterfly Shawl 48
    Cake Band 60
    Christening Gown 52
    Christening Photograph Album Cover 54
    Christening Photograph Frame 44
    Christening Sampler 62
couching 126
cross stitch, how to do 124
cushions
    scented wedding shoe 76
    wedding ring 80

## D
dress, bridesmaid's 84
Drawstring Bag 88

## E
Engagement Card 68
evenweave 122

## F
fabrics 122–3
Family Tree Sampler 108
Floral Birthday Card
Flower Gift Tag 28
French knots 125

## G
Gift Tags 26
    birthday cup cake 29
    bumble bee 28
    champagne bottle 29
    flower 28
    rattle 28
Golden Wedding Sampler 100
gown, christening 52

## H
half cross stitch 124
hemming 126
hoops 123

## J
Jewellery Box 34

## L
long stitch 124

**M**

materials 122–3

**N**

New-born Baby Card 10

**P**

photograph album covers
christening 54
wedding anniversary 112
photograph frames
christening 44
ruby wedding 104
wedding 92
plastic canvas 122
pressing embroidered fabric 123

**R**

Rattle Gift Tag 28
Ruby Wedding Photograph Frame 104

**S**

samplers
alphabets 116–19, 121
animal ark 16
christening 62
family tree 108
golden wedding 100
60th birthday 30

wedding bouquet 72
Scented Wedding Show Cushion 76
shawls
butterfly christening 48
teddy bear 12
Silver Wedding Card 98
60th Birthday Sampler 30
sizing up or down 123
slip stitch 126
Sports Theme Birthday Card 38
stitches 124–6

**T**

Teddy Bear Shawl 12
21st Birthday Card

**W**

washing embroidered fabric 123
waste canvas 122–3
wedding projects 66–95
Bridesmaid's Dress 84
Drawstring Bag 88
Engagement Card 68
Scented Wedding Shoe Cushion 76
Wedding Bouquet Sampler 72
Wedding Cake Card 70
Wedding Photograph Frame 92
Wedding Ring Cushion 80
*see also* anniversary projects

# Acknowledgments

I would like to say a special thank you to all the following for all their help and encouragement:

To my wonderful mother, Josephine Irureta, for all her help and support.

My true friend Barbara Farren for her patient stitching.

The excellent stitchers, without whom this book would never have been completed: Carolina Connor, Bridget Creely, Janet Francis, Sarah Hardie, Anne Hyne, Doreen James, Irene Mills, Bridget Perez, Linda Pettiford, Muna Reyal and Patricia Yeomans.

Jon Stewart for his great photography and Barbara Stewart for her wonderful props and excellent style.

To all the staff at Collins & Brown, especially Clare Churly, Sarah Hoggett and Simon Brockbank.

Last, but by no means least, my wonderful supportive husband Bill, for always being ready to help without being asked.